Endorsments

An easily readable gathering of practical helps for every leader to use in growing forward. An excellent resource. Allen R. Hunt, Nationally Syndicated Radio Talk Show Host, The Allen Hunt Show.

I feel compelled to return often to most every topic for further reflection, and to share them with developing leaders. Jeff has compiled 52 insightful and challenging readings on a broad range of leadership topics, while consistently reinforcing critical core themes of true leadership. Gregg A. Mooney, Vice President, Brown and Caldwell.

Jeff Armbruster's delightful book "Some Practical Lessons in Leadership" contains many insights about the capacity to inspire others. However, the theme that came through most fully to me is expressed by a comment that I once heard broadcast journalist Eric Sevareid make about President Harry Truman "It's the integrity of the man that I remember". Jeff Armbruster became my close friend during my younger years when we were in graduate school together. I see in this book the mature insights then nascent in the young man of long ago. David R. Maidment, Director, Center for Research in Water Resources, The University of Texas at Austin

Having been privileged to participate in one of Jeff Armbruster's leadership classes I can authoritatively say his new book "Some Practical Lessons in Leadership (Observations from Daily Life)" is the next best thing to being there. His book speaks extensively to the concept of servant leadership and whether you are the CEO of a company, a government executive or simply trying to lead your teenager through the perils of adolescence the principles in this book provide valuable lessons to live and grow by. Barbara W. Wainman.

As a former Army officer in combat and now a business owner, I am quick to agree with Jeff when he says "Leadership is about getting results." However, he also shows the reader how to get those results even more effectively through humility, service, integrity and spirituality. I believe his observations outline what is surely the very best approach to leadership I have seen. Fred Weil, President, Image Group of Georgia

In our fast paced world of unrelenting change, Jeff's lessons are a drink of cool water ...refreshing, wise, and filled with spirit, that lift us up to run the race again, and this time, no matter the outcome, to win. Shelley Price-Khatib, President, Mullins, Price, Khatib and Associates.

Armbruster's book on leadership is a must study. Jeff gets to the core with real life practical applications that we as servant leaders can use and apply everyday. James L. Cook, Jr., President, National Financial Services Group

Some Practical Lessons in Leadership

To Laura
I pray that in all you do,
personally and professionally,
you will . . .
Lead humbly & Serve graciously

you are blessed by God

JH

Some Practical Lessons in Leadership

Observations from Daily Life

Jeffrey T. Armbruster

Foreword by Robert (Dusty) Staub, II

First printing May 2010

ISBN 1-4392-6355-8

Cover design by Patti Armbruster

Photo on back cover by Patti DiRito

Printed by CreateSpace

Dedicated to my grandchildren
with the sincere hope they will each find the seeds
of leadership God planted within them
and allow those seeds to grow.

Contents

Acknowledgments

As you read the pages that follow, please understand that much of what you encounter is the result of what I have learned from others, the gifts they have generously shared or given me. Included in the list of those from whom I have learned much and to whom I am grateful and owe much is Laurel, my wife of four decades. She has endured much during that time, including addresses in six different states during our first twelve years of marriage as I pursued my career. Laurel has loved me unconditionally, taught me much, and challenged me often. Her insights are remarkable. She lifts me up when I am down, and brings me back to earth when I fly off on a tangent. She continues to give me gifts beyond what I deserve by simultaneously being my strongest supporter, most severe critic, and best friend. She makes me be a better person.

Our children, Amy and David, who both make their mom and dad very proud that they decided to become parents, have also provided incredible support and encouragement, along with their spouses, Dan and Patti. Thanks to each of them.

My parents, Frank and Jane Armbruster, provided not only a firm foundation for life, particularly by the admirable way they have lived their lives, they also have provided lifelong encouragement to grow and give. To them, I will always be thankful.

And there are so many other family members (both outlaws and in-laws) who have given me so much through their (and our) life experiences that trying to name them all would surely result in forgetting some. However, my sister-in-law Junie Brown does deserve special mention because she ploughed through my original manuscript, edited it

i

thoroughly, and challenged me to reach deeper and express my ideas more clearly. I owe her a huge thank you.

My daughter-in-law, Patti Armbruster, applied her artistic talents to the design and creation of the cover of this book. She has beautifully portrayed two of the most compelling messages that leaders must take to heart: their actions must be based on serving the needs of others and they must all be done with a humble heart. The layout of the interior of the book is also her handiwork. Thank you, Patti, for all the love and energy you have contributed to this project.

In addition, there are many, many friends who have loved and taught me much though their generosity and experiences. One of those dear friends, Father Larry McNeil, has had a huge impact on my life in so many ways. To him I will always be grateful.

I would be remiss if I were not to thank many former USGS associates, particularly those who took me under their wings and put up with my slow learning, and those with whom I have directly worked, taught, and crossed paths as a result of the USGS leadership program, for it is they whom I must credit for even starting this project several years ago. In particular, I am grateful to Jim Cook, Tom Buchanan, Jim Biesecker, Bob Hirsch, and Rolland Carter, who, throughout my career, gave me opportunities beyond what I deserved and who each taught me much. Very special thanks must be offered to Nancy Driver, Dianne Jeffries, Lew Wade, Jim Sturdevant, Cynthia Harris, Steve Bohlen, Betsy Daniel, and Jerry McMahon, USGS colleagues who agreed to be the initial troupe of instructors for the Leadership Program, who provided the core of excitement for those who participated from the outset, and many of whom continue to inspire emerging leaders at USGS. Each of them has been an inspiration in so many ways, and for whatever reason, they continued to encourage my efforts.

I have also had the honor of working with a wide range of clients as a consultant and, from them, I have learned much, and to them I am grateful.

And, finally, I am truly thankful for those with whom I share my faith; I have prayed with them and for them and they have prayed for me. Many of the insights shared here come from them.

Foreword

I have had the privilege of getting to know and work with Jeff Armbruster over the past ten years. He is a man of deep faith, bedrock values, vision, and deep compassion. Further, he is what he writes about, a true "servant leader." In this compelling and elegant book Jeff has distilled decades of research, hands-on work and practice in the realm of acting both as a leader and also developing leadership ability and capacity in others. He is, in the words of Dan Millman, "a peaceful warrior." That fits him well, for he is, as the great peace activist and leader Danaan Perry was, a warrior of the heart – bringing faith, hope, compassion and deep commitment to his work as well as to those he coaches and with whom he works.

As I read through Jeff's practical, open-hearted words and concepts an old English saying came to mind, "If you want the fruit of the tree, you have to go out on a limb." Jeff will take you as a reader out on a limb but only after first thoroughly grounding you in the deep roots of what it takes to be an exceptional leader. He helps you discover, for example, in chapter two "Human Being Drives Us to Lead" the dual sides of the coin of personal leadership effectiveness – one side composed of "doing" and the other of "being." In fact, his whole book is an exercise in how to balance human "being" with human "doing" – skillfully weaving together the Yin and the Yang of personal power and efficacy by starting with the deep roots of being an incarnate soul in a world of challenge and, paradoxically, grace.

Jeff's stories and examples are akin to a sudden flash of lightening, illuminating the psycho-spiritual-physical-emotional-philosophical landscape that composes the deep textured reality of leading effectively in a complex world.

I particularly appreciate his deep sense of the paradox of leadership: "Aggressive-Humility" and "Speak loudly without making a sound" as well as "Doing while Being." His sense of humor and deep compassion for those he meets and the encounters he shares are worth the price of admission in and of themselves. Yet the stories do far more than entertain and illuminate the leadership landscape, they also inform and offer a pathway and some clear guidelines on personal efficacy and interpersonal mastery. Jeff provides clear structures and insights, even offering near the end of his book a chapter called, "Daily Reminders" where he provides questions to assist the reader in re-affirming and strengthening core dimensions of being such as: loyalty, empathy, agape (love), dedication, energy, respect, strength and sensitivity, humility, integrity and passion. Illumination he provides, yes, but also clear sign-posts, generative structures and practical, hands-on methodology.

Jeff tells us in this book that "Leaders must love" if they are to be effective over the long haul. Indeed, without love there is only, ultimately, failed leadership and hollowness in the human being. He challenges the reader to focus on the emotional intelligence (EQ) drivers of followership and leadership effectiveness, offering clear guidelines and insights to support greater development of EQ. As Jeff reminds us, "Leadership is from the inside out" – it is the character and heart of the individual that determines the quality of the leadership. I also appreciate how Jeff reminds us that leaders are coaches and they are constantly learning by being "coached" by those around them – it is, in essence, a virtuous cycle of mutual learning, passion, engagement, caring and co-development.

Some Practical Lessons in Leadership is one of those rare books that enlightens as it inspires, informs as it challenges and provides practical guidance as it dives deeply into philosophy. It is a book that can be savored, one short chapter at a time – reading one chapter a day in a short period of time, while allowing the reader to absorb and take-in the deeper insights at his or her own pace. It is a book that invites the reader to "own it," to engage with it and also be free to make notes in the margins for later review and further reflection. I invite you to jump in with both feet; the plunge will refresh, renew, revitalize and re-engage heart, mind, body and soul.

Robert (Dusty) Staub, II

President, Staub Leadership International, A Division of EQIQ, Inc.

Author of *The 7Acts of Courage* and
The Heart of Leadership

Prologue

Learning Takes Many Forms

A helicopter pilot and his passenger were caught in a low-cloud, fog situation; visibility was terrible. Then Murphy's Law struck—the entire navigation system died. The pilot could see virtually nothing, and now there were no electronics to get him and his passenger to safety. He slowly moved forward, inching his way along, when, suddenly, there in front of him was a very tall office building. He grabbed a piece of paper and with a felt tip marker wrote in bold letters, "Where am I?" and held the note so people in the building could see. A crowd had already gathered to see the visitor outside their window. Someone inside got a piece of paper and wrote a note to the pilot that said, "You are in a helicopter!" With that the pilot smiled, waved goodbye to the folks in the building, and flew directly to the airport, where he landed safely.

The puzzled passenger asked how he managed to get back safely with all of the adverse weather when it was obvious to him that the reply the pilot got to his question was of no use at all. The pilot's answer surprised him more than just a little. The pilot said as soon as he saw the response to his question by the office workers, even though he knew they were technically correct and, further, he already knew what they told him, he was positive he had to be hovering outside the building where the customer service department of the *So & So Company* was located (he had previous experience working with that department). Once he knew what building he was near, he knew exactly how to get home.

We learn in a wide variety of ways. Some of us learn best by reading, others by experience or doing, some by

listening, and still others through instruction from experts—
and sometimes we learn valuable lessons even when we
are exposed to information that is technically correct but
seemingly not too useful, just like the helicopter pilot did.
I have learned by each of these methods at different times
of my life. However, in recent years, I have learned an
incredible number of useful leadership lessons by simply
being significantly more *aware* than ever before of what is
going on around me.

When I allow my antennae to be raised, to be in constant
receive mode, and to be tuned to the *learning frequency*, I am
amazed by the variety and depth of opportunities to learn
new things, gain new insights, and, in the process, hopefully
become a more effective person and a better leader. This book
is a record of some of the lessons I have learned about what
it means to be a leader through this heightened awareness,
and it represents a record of my increased consciousness
of my own leadership strengths and weaknesses. But how
and why I chose to record these observations requires
some explanation.

In the early 1990s, I began an extensive study of a
growing body of literature in the field of leadership and after
a while began receiving invitations to speak on a range of
leadership topics, mostly to U.S. Geological Survey (my
employer) audiences. The combination of reading, studying,
and speaking significantly enhanced my knowledge and
understanding of what it means to be a leader—and not too
surprisingly created a thirst to learn even more. I make no
claim that all that work and those insights have actually made
me a better leader. Such a judgment could only be made by
others. In fact, how could I (or we) ever legitimately claim
to do anything more than *practice* being a leader? From my
perspective, if I ever try to fool myself into believing I have
become the best leader I am capable of being, I have not
only lost perspective of what it really means to be a leader

but have also stopped trying. Leadership development is a lifelong process.

In 1998, I was asked by the director of the USGS to design and implement a Leadership Development Program for the agency. I jumped at the chance. The format of the program we designed was built around an intensive week of training by a variety of mostly in-house experts, each of whom was uniquely qualified by his or her experience to teach the sessions he or she taught. By the end of each week-long session, the participants and we, the instructors, were exhausted. Borrowing a sports metaphor, we worked hard not to leave anything on the field.

After each of the first two offerings of the class, called by some "Leadership 101" and by others "The Shepherdstown Experience," named for the training location, numerous participants asked if I would consider sending regular email notes to them to help them keep alive the excitement they developed during the program. They expressed concern they would lose the fire when they went back to their day jobs.

For about two and a half years, I sent out what I called "Leadership Follow-Up Thoughts." Each was simply an attributed quote from a wide range of published sources that I thought would be useful. I also hoped that providing the source reference would encourage folks to read, study, and learn even more. The common theme of the 120-plus weekly reminders was that each of us can be a true leader if we are willing to work hard, be dedicated to bedrock principles, care deeply about people, get up when we stumble and fall, and be committed to lifelong learning. But the underlying message in all the "Thoughts" was the importance of setting a good example, engaging in quality relationships, and being dedicated to the service of others—in short, reaching outside of ourselves to create value.

After more than two years of quoting the work of others in my continuing commitment to those who had come through our program, I decided I had a few ideas of my own that others might find useful. Why not share some of the lessons I had learned along the way? Why not try putting some warning signs on the potholes I had stumbled into? Why not share some of the lessons so generously shared with me by so many? So, I made up my mind that for the foreseeable future, I would continue my weekly encouragement to others (and learning for me) by creating what turned out to be a series of essays describing my observations on a wide range of leadership topics.

A consistent theme throughout the essays is the responsibilities of leaders to be role models, the need to be humble and live principle-centered lives, and an obligation to willingly serve the legitimate needs of others. These foundation blocks, which are fully consistent with my moral and religious beliefs, cannot be repeated too often. From the outset, I hoped that each topic would be useful to the readers in their work environment, but my unwritten rule while preparing each essay was to make the thoughts useful in all aspects of life—at work, at home, etc.

The observations that follow are the thoughts I wrote about and shared with my USGS colleagues and then client organizations. They were all written after I retired in August 2001. For the most part, they are in the order in which they were written. Each one pretty much stands alone and does not require reading the ones before. The topic each week was selected through a process of planned randomness—in other words, I wrote about something that seemed important to me at the time I sat down at my computer—and I must admit the topic often did not develop until I had started writing about one idea, which spawned the ultimate theme for that week's entry.

Somehow, I believe that each topic was inspired by the unknown (to me) need of others because nearly every week, multiple recipients would email back or call and say something like, "Have you been looking over my shoulder?" or "How did you know I needed to hear that today?" or "You really know my weak spots, don't you?" Of course, I always responded that I was looking over their shoulder, or just knew they needed to hear x or y, or "Yes, I do know your weak points!" Actually, I did say those things occasionally, but with tongue in cheek. The truth is that the topic selected each week was the one I most needed to hear myself—and being like most people, I should not have been surprised that others thought I was writing the piece especially for them.

The ideas I have tried to capture were inspired by something I read, a photograph I saw, a person I met or talked with, a talk, speech or sermon I heard, a situation I was faced with, an event I experienced, or some bit of wisdom that a family member or friend shared with me. So because I had committed to communicate with several hundred folks on a weekly basis, I had no other choice except to have my antennae raised and the learning frequency fine-tuned.

My fondest hope is that each of you who decide to read through one or more of the observations that follow will feel your time was wisely spent. I have titled the observations so you can quickly turn to a particular topic of interest or need. You can read them in any order you wish, skip a few if the topics are not relevant to you at this time, read them all in one sitting (although I would strongly advise against that!), read a few today, a few tomorrow, etc., or read just one a week—the way they were originally written. There is one for each week for a year. Regardless, I am honored that you would spend your valuable time with these words. Please feel free to share your ideas or experiences by contacting me at jtarmbru@bellsouth.net or visit www.jeffarmbruster.com.

Observation

1

Speak Loudly Without Making a Sound

Several years ago, I observed a very talented young colleague make her first leadership training presentation. She was extremely well prepared, had all of her material highly organized, and looked and sounded the part of a seasoned professional. Her words were carefully selected and put together, and skillfully delivered. I watched and listened with delight at her successful debut. In a casual debriefing later, however, she admitted that she did not feel that she had landed the resounding 'punch' she had hoped for. She felt something was missing.

What she had experienced is pretty common for leaders in any endeavor. And like a true leader, she wanted feedback on what she could do better or differently that would allow her to be more effective the next time she taught or had to give a talk. I asked her a very simple question that one of my life teachers had asked me many years ago when I found myself in a similar situation: "When you were making your presentation, how many people in the audience did you make eye contact with?" (The question could just as easily have been, "In your role as a leader, when you were talking with Mary/Joe, did you make eye contact with her/him?")

Genuine leaders know their eyes do more than allow them to just see things around them. Our eyes also serve as windows to our souls. Think about it—when you are talking with someone and not making strong eye contact, you cannot

1

convey your thoughts and feelings fully. You are cheating the person with whom you are communicating because you are choosing not to use all available avenues of getting your message across. What they receive is only the verbal part and that might constitute no more than ten to twenty percent of the message you intend. In fact, intonation, body language, etc. usually account for the largest part of the message we are sharing during face-to-face conversation, and much of the nonverbal message is carried through facial expression and eye contact.

Both the sincerity of the message we are trying to convey and the truth of our feelings for the other person are masked unless we speak with them using what I think of as the silent but significantly meaningful *language of the eyes*. By engaging in strong eye-to-eye contact, we are far more likely to be involved in true heart-to-heart conversation than if we are checking out the condition of the toes of our shoes! If we want others to know who we really are and what we really feel, we must be willing to take a risk and open up by looking them in the eye.

For many of us, making eye contact is extremely uncomfortable and requires us to consciously and courageously override an often well-developed habit of looking away from those we are talking with. When speaking to a group or teaching a class, the tendency to look away rather than at people is even stronger. For a wide range of reasons, many of us choose to keep our guard up, rather than being fully open. We choose to be risk averse and protect ourselves rather than allowing ourselves to be vulnerable.

Our eyes divulge our true thoughts and feelings most of the time. If you are having a tough time understanding this concept, tune in to one of the many televised championship poker tournaments that are popular today. Many of the participants play cards with their eyes hidden behind very dark lenses, so as not to divulge any of their thoughts or feelings about the cards they are playing, and thus give competitors even a small advantage over them. Even experienced actors find it difficult to lie with their eyes. By contrast, if we hope to be effective leaders and have truly meaningful conversation with others, we must be willing to exchange our thoughts and feelings fully, not just with the words out of our mouths, but with the even greater number of unspoken words we share with our eyes.

Being vulnerable is uncomfortable for most of us, because throughout our lives we have learned to protect ourselves. And we must also acknowledge that for some people, cultural norms discourage direct eye contact. But while it can be risky, there is a tremendous payoff for consciously making eye contact with others. They will sense our vulnerability and see our honesty and good intentions if we keep the windows to our heart open. We in turn will be rewarded by the honesty and sincerity they show us in return.

During her second outing, my young friend did all of the preparation she had done the first time, but this time, she also mustered the courage to actively engage the audience with riveting eye contact, first one person, then another, and then another. The impact this time was everything that she (and those in the class) had hoped for. She hit the metaphorical *grand slam*. So whether you are talking with just one person, a group, or with a large crowd, let others see who you really are by allowing them to see *you* through your eyes. Your ability to lead and influence others will surely increase.

I had the pleasure recently of having dinner with her and several other former colleagues and can attest she is even better at engaging the listener visually than before. She has become a truly amazing leader in her own right and a wonderful communicator. She now speaks loudly, without making a sound, by skillful use of the *language of the eyes*.

Observation

2

Our Human 'Being' Drives Us to Lead

Psychologists for years have said that we are made up of four parts—the physical, mental, social/emotional and spiritual. Stephen Covey (*The 7 Habits of Highly Effective People*) and others have recently written about the importance of those four dimensions of our humanity. Because I am a very visual person, trained as an engineer (and, yes, I know many of you think engineers are weird), I like to visualize concepts using pictures or diagrams. The mental picture I have always used to represent this psychological concept is a pie chart, with the entire pie being cut into four pieces.

That picture made very good sense to me for a long time, but I recently decided my mental model was incomplete and too simplistic because we humans are far too complex to be represented by a single, flat, two-dimensional surface. I tried to come up with a three-dimensional image to add what seemed like the appropriate complexity and thus a more accurate picture, but had to settle for a quasi three-dimensional one, that of a coin. Think of a coin as a two-sided pie chart with some substance in between.

Which of the four parts of our humanity should be on one side of the coin and which ones on the other, and how are the two sides related to one another? After some reflection, I decided that my original model was okay as far as showing that all four parts must remain on one side because they

4

really do make up the whole of us, or at least one 'view' of our wholeness.

So one side of the coin would have all four parts. But what about the other side? What does it represent and how does this more complex model provide added insight to our understanding of ourselves and our effective leadership?

After much consideration about what it really means to be a leader, I was forced to conclude that the additional, needed description of our wholeness (the flip side of my coin model) should be made up of only two components—the *doing* part of us and the *being* part of us. These two parts are intimately connected to each other and to the components on the 'flip side' in some complex way through the substance in between the two surfaces. I am not smart enough to fully describe those complex relationships, but fortunately a complete linkage is not critical to my point here. What I do know is leadership is clearly about action, not the position we hold. It reflects what we actually DO. But possibly the most important part of leadership is about who we *are* inside— our *being* part. Our *being* is our core. Getting and staying in touch with our core is the essence of our human *being*, which ultimately guides and gives purpose to our human *doing*. I consider this insight to be critical to an overall understanding of what it means to be a leader.

Someone who immediately comes to mind as a person whose human *doing* was guided by her human *being* is 1979 Nobel Prize for Peace winner Mother Theresa of Calcutta. Virtually everyone in the world knows about her, but the poorest of the poor from the streets of Calcutta clearly know her best. She cared for them, nurtured them and loved them when no one else did. In her Nobel Prize acceptance speech she said: "I choose the poverty of our poor people. But I am grateful to receive (the Nobel) in the name of the hungry, the naked, the homeless, of the crippled, of the blind, of the lepers, of all those people who feel unwanted, unloved, uncared-for throughout society, people that have become a burden to the society and are shunned by everyone." Her actions to help the poor are a vivid and clear reflection of who she was down to the very core of her being. Her core was made up of a genuine desire to do God's work—to love, to do good, to be fully present, and to lift up the needs of others. She was fully connected to the core of her humanity and spent every waking moment living it out. In very simple terms, Mother Theresa was dedicated to allowing her human *being* to guide her human *doing*.

You may argue that Mother Theresa is an exception, or at least an exceptional person. But is she? My guess is that she herself would deny being such, but she would admit to being highly disciplined and sharply focused. In fact, she said frequently that she did nothing exceptional, only ordinary things with exceptional love. We can learn many valuable lessons from her example that will help us live up to our leadership potential.

As leaders, what does it mean to get in touch with and stay in touch with our human *being*, our core? I believe it means that we must know who we are and what we want to be. Such knowledge and intention require a great deal of self-assessment and reflection and unusual honesty. The logical starting point in my leadership journey might very well be to ask myself, "What makes me tick?" Am I guided by selflessness and love or am I mostly looking out for *number one*? Am I mostly about serving others, or about being served? Am I motivated to spend my energy helping others, or am I holding back so as not to overexert myself? Do I give it all I have, or do I have some left over at the end of the day? Other similar questions could be posed, but you get the idea.

Only when we get to know ourselves better can we begin to understand what motivates our actions. Only when we constantly challenge ourselves to do more will we realize that we still have so much more to give. Some researchers have shown that most geniuses use only a small part of the brain power they have, and those of us not as gifted actually use less than half of what we have. Most of us who strive and work hard to be leaders are still leaving a lot on the field—but for what purpose? For those like Mother Theresa (and others), who gave (and still give) so much, each would almost surely attest they reaped huge returns on their investment of energy in the service of others that far exceeded the cost. What a deal!

In very simple terms, being a leader requires that we know our inner selves well, continually strive to know ourselves even better, be of strong moral character, be highly disciplined, and act on the very finest of motivations that emanate from our core. A clear understanding of our human *being* guides and gives noble purpose to our human *doing*. No one can ever ask you to do more. Are you ready to *really* get to know who you are?

Observation

3

Leadership Is Hard, But...

⬥⬥⬥

The opening words of M. Scott Peck's famous book, *The Road Less Traveled*, are: "Life is difficult." When I first read those words some years ago, my immediate reaction was, "How odd to begin a book with such a somber thought." But I have come to realize the truth in his statement. Life *is* difficult. Yet as Peck points out, "Once we truly understand and accept it—then life is no longer difficult. Because once it is accepted, the fact that life is difficult no longer matters." As a friend of mine likes to say, "It is what it is."

Leadership, too, is difficult, but the rewards are significant—whether we lead on the personal level, in a small group, organizationally, or beyond. In fact, leadership is so rewarding that our lives will be greatly enriched merely because of the journey.

Developing our leadership capabilities requires that we get in touch and stay in touch with our heart, the very core of our being. But let us be clear—doing so is difficult for many, particularly for those, including myself, who have developed a high opinion of themselves (i.e. "legends in their own mind"), who have achieved a high level of success in business, government or academia, and who are highly analytical in the way they look at life and solve problems. Unfortunately, such people often lack relationship skills.

Real leadership requires that we look at and treat others as people who have wants, needs, desires, and aspirations at least as important as our own, not less. So often, particularly as we ascend the ladder of success, we expect that our importance, our position, our very lot in life implies that we are worthier than others and should be served. Yet leadership demands just the opposite. The further up the totem pole we are, the greater our obligation to reach out (and down) to others in a spirit of service. And regardless of how analytical we might be, or how successful we think we are and no matter how few natural talents we might think we have in the *human dimension*, we have the obligation to connect with, empathize with, and serve others.

In their book, *Breakpoint and Beyond—Mastering the Future*, Today, husband and wife George Land and Beth Jarman advise leaders:

We have the opportunity to significantly change our minds about how we relate and connect with one another. Our suggestion is to shift immediately to the belief that we are all interconnected. If we accept this reality, we will shift the way we communicate with one another. We have the potential to interact in a spirit of trust, openness, and honesty. And perhaps with an ecology of the human spirit we will move to true interdependence throughout this magnificent planet where we reside...

The beliefs of many people run directly opposite to what we're advocating. [But] we know that once you make the decision, your interactions and relationships with others immediately change. If you are trustworthy, you'll be trusted. If you connect based on trying to create a profound win for everyone, others sense the shift. This natural way of connecting with people has profound consequences for good. Try it! And stay with it. Find out for yourself.

Leadership dictates that we come face-to-face with the reality that no matter where we are, no matter what we are doing, we can have a positive impact on those around us. We can choose to treat others with dignity and respect, or not. We can choose to be others-centered or self-centered. We can choose to look down our noses at those who are below us on the organizational chart or we can work tirelessly on their behalf. We can choose to ignore the needs of others or we can view the needs of others as our invitation to do everything we can to help them. Leadership is hard because it demands that we use our energy to lift others up through serving them.

Leadership calls us to be all that we were created to be. The spirit of genuine leadership should nag us constantly, encouraging us to be courageously in touch with both our own feelings and those of others. We all have the ability to lead; we all have the responsibility to lead. But doing so requires conscious choices on our part. Will I serve? Will you serve? Or not?

Observation

4

Know What You Stand For

⚭

Each of us has a value system—a set of beliefs, ideals, guidelines that we live by. Our values are formed, expanded, and reshaped over a lifetime and are influenced by the people and experiences of our lives. Knowing this, what should our value system be made up of so that it serves us well, particularly in difficult times?

I have found it quite useful to think about my value system as a toolbox (note: another one of my mental models) filled with tools that will help me with relationships, self-awareness, behavior, and life in general. Each of us gets to choose the tools we put in our toolbox. Metaphorically, however, the tools that it makes the most sense to select are the high-quality ones that come with a lifetime guarantee. I believe the tools guaranteed to help us lead useful, productive, worthwhile lives are what Stephan Covey calls "bed rock" principles. He describes principles as "guidelines for human conduct that are proven to have enduring, permanent value. They are fundamental, unarguable, self evident and universally applicable. Principles are not invented by us or by our society; they are the laws of the universe that pertain to human relationships and human organizations."

There are essential principles that should be put into everyone's values 'toolbox' because they are so important in guiding our daily lives. Some that come immediately to mind (and this list is far from exhaustive) are honesty, integrity, humility, service to others, recognizing and valuing the dignity of other people, charity, justice, and observing and nurturing the potential in others. No doubt you can add to your list. Interestingly, each of the principles listed here is also an important characteristic for being a good leader!

Honesty is one of the most obvious and important 'bedrock' principles that characterize principle-centered leaders, and most people agree that honesty should be a part of the fabric that makes us who we are. But, occasionally, I find someone who will argue that honesty should not always be our goal. In fact, some even contend there are occasions when we should not be honest. There may be such occasions, but I have never known a situation when dishonesty is appropriate and frankly I do not believe such occasions exist! If we allow ourselves to slip into believing that a violation of such a principle is justified in small matters, I would suggest that we are putting ourselves onto what a dear friend of mine calls a "slippery slope." If violating the principle is okay this time, when will it be okay again? Are there situations, times, or places where we can be dishonest and still consider ourselves principle-centered? I don't think so.

In much the same way that ethics require us to always consider the impact our actions have on others, being principle-centered requires us not to allow ourselves to be seduced into actions that violate our very nature. Dedication to the truth, as we best know it, is a vital part of personal discipline, and is required of those who would have others follow them. Does that mean we have the right to speak any truth that crosses our mind? The answer is, "Absolutely not." A former colleague and friend told me one time that her grandfather advised her, "You must always tell the truth, but you don't always have to be telling it."

As leaders, we must always be dedicated to telling the truth. But, as leaders, we must use good judgment when deciding what to talk about. We do not have the right most of

12

the time, for example, to divulge a confidence, even if we are telling the truth. Likewise, we have no right to use truthful information with the intent of hurting others.

Being a leader requires that we be an example for those around us—be a role model. Albert Schweitzer said, "Example is not the most important way to influence others. It is the only way." So how better to influence others than by leading a principle-centered life, using the tools in our toolbox—at home, at work, while alone, with friends— knowing full well that doing so creates a profound daily challenge for each us? Is there any evidence of "wear" on the tools you have in your value-system toolbox?

Observation

5

Leading Is Not the Same as Managing

People who choose to become managers sooner or later face the dilemma of balancing the differing responsibilities of manager and leader. John Kotter, Peter Drucker, and others have written much about the differences between leaders and managers. Still, there is often confusion when trying to work through the day-to-day responsibilities associated with each.

So how does a person balance the task-oriented, system-focused, bottom-line functions they must execute in the role of manager against the top-line, emotional, heart-centered focus of leader? From my perspective, everyone is called to be a leader, if in no other arena than in one-on-one situations (although many are called to lead in team and organizational settings and beyond), and some of those leaders are called to step forward to be managers. When taking on a management role, however, one cannot leave behind the responsibilities of leadership. I believe the very best managers take their leadership responsibilities quite seriously, while taking on the additional burdens of being a manager. To successfully execute the responsibilities of *leader-manager*, I believe there are two characteristics that are of paramount importance— humility and service.

A humble leader does not have to advertise his/her importance when he/she steps into a managerial role. Instead, a humble leader-manager identifies with the weakest member of his or her team. The leader-manager does not have to let others know about the power she or he has. Instead, she gets the job done while being empathetic to current realities of all sorts. He does not impose his will; rather he patiently waits for others to willingly follow. People will nearly always follow someone who leads by example rather than manages by decree. You see, humility is a disciplined strength, not a weakness or passivity.

What does it mean to be servant in the context of being a manager? Leader-managers are those who have the responsibility for getting things done, but they understand in their hearts that people, rather than machines or processes, are the doers. With such recognition, they dedicate much of their physical and emotional energy to helping followers by nurturing them, removing roadblocks, facilitating interactions, providing resources, etc. In short, leader-managers show how much they care by unconditionally serving followers' legitimate needs.

Contrast humble, service-driven leader-managers with some of the high-level executives in our country today, who have chosen to look out for their own personal financial gain at the expense of others. How many made headlines during the last few years of the twentieth century and the first few years of the twenty-first? While I am sure a comprehensive inventory has been compiled somewhere, we need recall only a few cases such as Enron, WorldCom, Global Crossing, HealthSouth, Fannie Mae, Freddie Mac, and others to understand the point. Each case highlights just how the drive for personal power and financial wealth dominated the thinking and actions of a few executives with the result being a severe negative impact on the welfare of many. These executives ignored the financial, organizational, and psychological fallout from their choices or considered it irrelevant or unimportant. How sad for the many who were hurt by the actions of a few.

Fortunately, there are leader-managers in all sorts of

organizations who take their responsibilities seriously, and the results speak for themselves. Interestingly, most do not make the headlines and a case could be made that most honorable leaders seldom, if ever, even make the news. The real leader-managers are the ones who not only get the job done, but also honor the humanity of those doing the work by removing unnecessary roadblocks for them and by concentrating on developing and maintaining high quality relationships with them. When followers know in their heads and hearts that their leader-manager would crawl through the metaphorical fire for them, even though they get zero recognition, rest assured everyone will know who has authority, who has power, who has position. All will know — and willingly follow!

Observation

6

Regret Is Debilitating

Leaders have the huge responsibility of being role models to those around them, yet they are faced with the same day-to-day trials and challenges as everyone else.

A friend recently asked what I thought was one of the most debilitating emotions to which we could allow ourselves to fall prey. After reeling off several I thought were troublesome (and my friend agreed to each one I mentioned), I sensed I had not hit upon the one he was thinking about. So I asked him to share his thoughts. His response surprised me, yet when reflecting on his premise, I had to wholeheartedly agree with him that *regret* can cripple our ability to be effective leaders. "Regret simply drags us down," my friend graciously offered.

No matter how much we might regret an action, circumstance, or inaction, nothing can change the past. What value is there in plaguing our hearts with a debilitating string of "if onlys," knowing that no matter what our current desires or capabilities might be, we cannot reverse the clock and change what has already happened? "You see," he offered, "regret can make you hard and mistrustful." Regret can also negatively impact a healthy sense of self-worth.

His last statement got me thinking a lot about how regret could cause negative repercussions, which in turn could impact one's ability to lead. How effective a leader would or could I be if I allowed my heart to harden? The fact is I could not establish, nourish, and maintain high-quality relationships with a hardened spirit, so my ability to lead would be significantly diminished because leadership is fundamentally about connecting with others in healthy, productive ways. How effective would I be if I did not trust those around me? The answer to this question screams the obvious—without trust, I would not allow myself to enter into relationships and my unwillingness to trust would be matched, in kind, by the unwillingness of others to trust me.

We cannot be effective leaders when our hearts are hard and our relationships mistrustful and strained. As trite as it might sound, most of us have a remarkable capacity to rise above disappointments and turn them into valuable life lessons. With a little practice and careful consideration, we can and must courageously resolve to learn from our experiences then creatively choose how to move forward.

Rather than dwelling on a disappointing outcome and slipping into the regret pit when things do not materialize the way we had hoped, we can follow the advice of Roz and Ben Zander (*The Art of Possibility*) by consciously stopping and saying, "How fascinating. What can I learn from this experience?" I frequently provide this suggestion to coaching clients and leadership development classes as a way of helping them deal with disappointments and misfortune, and they nearly always look at me as though I had three heads. The fact is, though, it works. Those of you who are skeptical should give it a try. Doing this little exercise will at least put a smile on your face, and your smile alone will help put you in a better frame of mind and heart. None of us has the ability to change the past, but each of us has the opportunity and ability to create our present and future.

Rather than wallowing in regret for something we did or did not do, say, or think, why not make restitution, if only to ourselves, by making decisions and taking actions that will satisfy and reset our internal compass? Once we have done so, we are free to move on with the resolve to avoid the same pitfalls in the future. "How fascinating. What can I learn from this experience?"

Observation

7

Leaders Develop Others

⁂

Leaders must *serve* those they lead. Robert Greenleaf, in his seminal work, *Servant Leadership*, talks about the many ways of serving. One of those ways is focused on the principle of looking for and developing the potential in others. That sounds a bit lofty; what does it really mean? It means that a leader has the responsibility to help identify the talent and potential of all those he leads and then help them to become the very best they are capable of being — often by challenging them to grow beyond their own perceived limits.

One way we can nurture those we lead is to ask them to take on responsibilities that force them to stretch significantly. Another way is to ensure that they are put into high visibility positions where others will be able to observe their performance. Also, nurturing leaders know when to teach, when to advise, when to prod, and when to simply listen and observe. They know that *leaders-in-training* must be given the freedom to explore, make mistakes, fall, and pick themselves up so that the can learn from the setback. Nurturing leaders know in their hearts that tight reins seldom produce a new generation of trusting leaders who will in turn nurture others and so they willingly take reasonable risks when delegating and assigning responsibilities. They offer encouragement when the follower stumbles, and they are quick to acknowledge success.

These ideas clearly apply to the workplace, but in truth, like most leadership concepts, they apply to life in general. For example, parents who are leaders allow their children to explore and grow and encourage them to take responsibility, while holding them accountable for their actions.

Early in my lengthy career in federal service, I was fortunate to have had several servant-leaders take a deep and abiding interest in my development, giving me challenging technical assignments, exposing me to influential technical and managerial types in the organization, and nudging me to accept transfers that allowed my career to develop in ways that would not have been possible had I stayed in the comfortable office where my professional life began. To each of them I am eternally grateful. One such leader in particular provided me opportunities well beyond what I likely deserved. I find it interesting, but not surprising, that most willing followers who want to learn will rise to the expectations of those who took a chance on them, even when the expectations are a huge stretch.

Some years ago I had the opportunity to select a young man to lead an important research project. My boss (who was the approving official) was dead set against my choice. Although the person I selected had never led such an effort, my gut told me he could do the job even though he did not have a proven track record. In the end, my boss approved my choice. The new manager asked me what was expected of him, and did I have any advice for his success. With very similar advice my early mentors gave me, I told him, "Your job is to serve the people assigned to your project, and give them the freedom to use their professional judgment in carrying out their work. You have responsibility for completing the work and will be held accountable for the results. I will stay out of your hair—but if you need anything, just let me know."

His team finished their work on time, their project reports were ahead of schedule, and the quality of their results was excellent. This young manager became an extremely competent leader-manager and, he, in turn, has nurtured many other young leader-managers into higher-level roles.

Please understand, however, that when you develop a person to his or her full potential, he or she will be sought after, and possibly even be hired away. The possibility must be realized and accepted in advance. But if you choose not to develop that person fully you will constantly be holding them back and that is a lose-lose proposition no matter how you view it—both for the person and the organization. Servant-leaders salve the sting of their loss with the comfortable knowledge that they have done their best for their student and his or her growth.

In their highly respected book, *The Leadership Challenge*, Jim Kouzes and Barry Posner state:

When leaders share power with others, they're demonstrating profound trust in and respect of others' abilities. Leaders create a covenant when they help others to grow and develop, and that help is reciprocated. People who feel capable of influencing their leaders are more strongly attracted to those leaders and more committed to effectively carrying out their responsibilities. They own their jobs. The leader who is most open to influence, who listens, and who helps others is the leader who is most respected and most effective—not, as traditional management myth has it, the highly controlling, 'tough-guy boss.' By showing respect, leaders build up credit that can be drawn upon later when they ask constituents to stretch for ever-higher levels of performance.

Servant-leaders, as a result, become transformational leaders. Are you regularly helping others achieve all they are capable of being? Are you helping transform the lives of others by the life you live?

Observation

8

The Power of Vision

Creating a compelling vision is one of the most important responsibilities of a leader. Vision, among other things, generates a sense of hope. Hope, in turn, is particularly needed by leaders (and followers, alike) during unsettling times or in difficult circumstances. In his bestseller, *Emotional Intelligence*, Daniel Goleman states that modern researchers are finding that

> Hope does more than offer a bit of solace amid affliction; it plays a surprisingly potent role in life, offering an advantage in realms as diverse as school achievement and bearing up in onerous jobs. Hope, in a technical sense, is more than the sunny view that everything will turn out all right. C. R. Snyder (1991) defines it with more specificity as 'believing you have both the will and the way to accomplish your goals, whatever they may be.'

Hope compels us to move forward through difficulties while keeping us buoyed above the turbulence of daily life. Those who lack hope often see themselves as victims, see little or no way to solve the difficult problems life throws at them, and generally concentrate on the conditions that prevent them from overcoming troublesome situations. By contrast, those who are hopeful tend to see themselves as capable of solving problems, look for opportunities to be innovative, and tend to see the light at the end of the tunnel when dealing with difficult events in their lives. In such ways, we have an amazing amount of power to create our own realities.

Goleman concludes:

> From the perspective of emotional intelligence, having hope means that one will not give in to overwhelming anxiety, a defeatist attitude, or depression in the face of difficult challenges or setbacks. Indeed, people who are hopeful evidence less depression than others as they maneuver through life in pursuit of their goals, are less anxious in general, and have fewer emotional distresses.

The connection between vision and hope is attitude. Knowing where we are headed and being hopeful about getting there happens most effectively when we choose our attitude, versus having our attitude determined for us by others, or by the events or circumstances around us. The attitude that we have at any given moment is the one we choose to have—and that is a near-gospel truth.

Many organizations develop lofty workplace vision statements. Some actually pursue their vision; many others use them as framed artwork on the office walls or in the main lobby, or as filler for their web sites. Still other organizations are far less articulate but use their visions in extraordinary ways. One such organization is the Pike Place Fish Market in Seattle, Washington. Their vision is very simple and, as a result, they actually renamed the business to reflect their vision—*World Famous Pike Place Fish*. Their company name IS their company vision! Everyone and everything associated with the fish market is dedicated to living up to the "World Famous" part of their name.

At the time they did the renaming, they were barely a half-step away from financial disaster. When everyone began to live the name, they actually became what they said they were. All decisions and actions are now based on the vision, in good times and in tough times. The sense of hope, excitement, and vitality that surrounds the market is both magical and contagious. The fishmongers live by a creed of "choosing your attitude"—the rest follows (see *When Fish Fly* by John Yokoyama and Joseph Michelli).

But even three millennia ago, Solomon (Proverbs 29:18) wisely observed that "the people without vision will soon perish." Vision is important because it provides the foundation of hope—and hopefulness is part of both emotional and spiritual health.

Do you know clearly where you want to go?

Observation

9

How You Say What You Say Matters

The words we use to convey our thoughts and feelings to others speak volumes about us as leaders. But the way we communicate is even more telling. How we say things matters. Depending on which research results you review or believe, as much as ninety-five percent or fifty percent of the message we deliver to others is transferred by non-verbal signs such as body language, intonation, eye contact, etc. For example, communications steeped in empathy can warm the coolest of relationships. By contrast, if our verbal exchanges with others are sarcastic, regardless of the actual words we speak, our sarcasm bleeds through. (Interestingly, the word "sarcasm" comes from the same root word that means to "rip the flesh off of.")

Sarcasm can be quite hurtful and disruptive, and can cause thick walls to be built between people. Sarcasm often starts out as humor; unfortunately, it too often gets out of hand. In extreme cases, the author of sarcastic comments, in the guise of being funny (gone bad), purposefully uses his or her comments to hurt others. Sarcastic comments can "rip the flesh off of" people's feelings—they can "rip the flesh off of" relationships. So why do people wield this weapon? Why take something that could be fun (humor), and use it as a weapon (sarcasm)?

In my opinion, pride is the root cause of sarcasm. Think about it. How better to lift myself up (relative to you) than to put you down? How better to show my own superiority than to show you your mediocrity? How better to highlight my intelligence than to spotlight your lack of it?

I would like to say that I have been a model practitioner of the ideas presented here. But the truth is that in my own stumbling through life, I have managed to say far too many things that were hurtful to others. In some cases, I intended to hurt. I deeply regret those times and am genuinely sorry for having been so thoughtless. But most of the time, when I have hurt others by what I have said, I did not mean for that to happen—but it did, unintentionally—often to those I love the most. I strive now never to hurt others with my words, intentionally or unintentionally, but it is not easy to break old habits. And the old expression about the 'road to hell being paved with good intentions' seems to be alive and well.

Leaders have many opportunities to influence others by the way they communicate. In group settings, for example, effective leaders use chances to speak as opportunities to build up, enhance, ask for, and add clarification to dialogue. By contrast, weak leaders (or non-leaders) use their floor time to belittle, berate, or drop bomblets (of a variety of sorts, for a wide range of reasons) into a conversation for the purpose of throwing the proceedings off track. As leaders, we each have the responsibility to serve the best interests of others through our words, the way we convey our words, and through our demeanor.

My point here is quite simple—what we say and how we say it makes a big difference in our ability to communicate as leaders or in our effectiveness as spouses, parents, relatives, friends, etc. What we say and how we say it can make a huge difference in the quality of the relationships we have. Leaders do not need to be articulate, oratorical geniuses, but we do need to speak and listen empathetically with and from both our hearts and our heads. We do not need to be clever "wordsmiths," we need to be genuine—because others sense the quality of our character through our genuineness.

Our communications with others must reflect an authentic, sincere recognition that their wants, needs, and aspirations are as important as our own. When we set a good example by our actions in the way we communicate, others will quickly pick up on our high level of interest in and concern for them—and respond in kind!

Are you setting a positive example and building bridges with others by what you say and how you say it—or are you tearing them down and creating anxiety? Are you part of the solution, or part of the problem? Only you can choose.

Observation

10

Leaving a Legacy

⚯

Every now and then, life throws us a curve ball. I was reminded of that recently when a dearly loved relative died rather suddenly. She had lived a long, hard but full and rewarding life. At her funeral, I gave one of the two eulogies and the other was given by one of her daughters. As I prepared my remarks, I could not help but reflect on the legacy that each of us builds as we journey through life. Her legacy included the five wonderful daughters she raised and educated to be vibrant, contributing members of society; the positive impact she made on the lives of two generations of children she taught during her career; and the wonderful stories she shared with young and old alike.

I read somewhere years ago that "the legacy we leave is the life we lead." I remember wondering at the time just what that really meant. After reflecting on that challenge, I have come to conclude that our legacy is composed primarily of what we do that positively impacts the lives of others. Here are a few questions that could help each of us decide whether we are on the right path to building a worthy legacy:

- Do I always do what I believe is right?
- Do I seek to serve others rather than expecting to be served?
- Do I use my energy to build others up rather than tear them down?

- Do I treat others with dignity and respect regardless of how they treat me?
- Do I listen with the intent of really hearing what others say?
- Am I ethical in all my dealings, regardless of the circumstances?
- Do I selflessly share the gifts I have been given with others?
- Do I look for the good in others?
- Am I actively helping those less fortunate than I?

Clearly this list is far from exhaustive, but I think you get the point.

The life we lead—whether we do so as a stay-at-home parent, a world-class scientist, a middle manager, a teacher, an accountant, an executive, a member of the clergy, whatever—is full of opportunities to enrich the lives of those around us. How we choose to use our abilities in the service of others will determine just what kind of legacy we leave—the kind of person we really are. Likewise, the kind of person we are directly influences the kind of leader we become.

I frequently use an exercise designed around a story Stephen Covey tells in his *The 7 Habits of Highly Effective People*, in a section on "Principles of Personal Leadership." Covey asks the reader to visualize what you eventually come to realize is your own funeral. A family member, a friend, a colleague, and a member of your faith community will get up to talk about what you meant to them. Covey asks the simple question, "What would you like each of these speakers to say about you and your life?" I invite you to think about doing this exercise right now, because if you take it seriously, the exercise can be life-altering. I often ask folks to repeat the same exercise on a regular basis as a way of reflecting on their personal growth and development. I often do, and find that much additional work is still needed.

31

Are you, right now, doing what is needed to leave the legacy you intend? If so, great. If not, the time to begin (or begin again) is now. Tomorrow, quite simply, may be too late.

Observation

11

Say "Thank You" Often

Two of the most powerful words anyone can say are *thank you*—and saying those words is even more important for leaders. Many would suggest saying *thank you* is just good manners, but in reality, it is far more than that. A sincere expression of gratitude for a kindness, for being served, for a gift, for support of any kind is also an act of thoughtfulness and humility. Leaders—whether they are leading up, leading down, or leading peers, whether they are at home, work, or out and about, whether with family, friends, colleagues, or strangers—have numerous opportunities each day to lift others up and honor them with this simple phrase.

Thank you, when said with genuineness, sends the messages "I value you," "I appreciate you," and "My relationship with you is important." Even when you thank a perfect stranger, you send a loud, clear message about who they are and who you are as a person. How better to let someone know how you appreciate them than to acknowledge their presence, their humanity, their inherent value?

We have all had the uplifting experience of being acknowledged by another for a kindness we have shown, and we know how good it feels. Similarly, we have each had the experience of either not being recognized with thanks, or, maybe even worse, had the *thank you* delivered with sarcasm, animosity, or insincerity. Such a negative experience is hurtful and can provoke any of us to anger,

33

instill disappointment, or even cause us to question our own self-worth. Regardless of who we are, who we are with, what position or rank we might hold, or the situation we are in, a *sincere thank you*, particularly when said to another while making direct eye contact, is powerful medicine for the human spirit. I cannot think of a situation when this act of courtesy, thoughtfulness, and humility is inappropriate.

No matter how busy we might find ourselves, saying *thank you* with an open heart will never infringe on our time. Our expression of appreciation to another could be the most important words they hear today! As leaders, taking the time to say *thank you* to followers will yield enormous returns. Just think: You have the power to help them "make a good day."

I offer a friendly challenge—before the end of the day today, thank someone for what they do, even if you have never spoken to them before. Then make the practice a many-times-a-day habit.

Observation

12

Emotional Intelligence Is Critical for Leaders

Numerous researchers have, over the past few decades, looked into the reasons executives fail. Investigator after investigator has developed and tested hypotheses, but virtually all have concluded that most executives who fail do not do so because of deficiencies in their IQ, business acumen, or technical prowess; they nearly always fail because of low emotional intelligence.

So what, exactly, is "emotional intelligence" and why is it so important? My definition of emotional intelligence is the ability to know yourself well (including an ongoing effort to know yourself better), to discipline yourself, and to develop, nourish, and maintain high-quality relationships.

Let's look at a bit of anecdotal evidence. In your work life, when was the last time you were asked how you "feel" about an issue (rather than what you "think")? When was the last time you asked someone about their feelings on an issue? Has someone totally missed a nonverbal message you recently conveyed?

What about your powers of observation: Do you readily sense the feelings of others from the expressions on their faces, the way they stand or sit, the tones of their voices? Has someone misinterpreted your message to the point that they might have surprised you by responding with aggression or anger? Are you quick to ask clarifying questions when you hear something that seems inappropriate, out-of-character, or out of proportion? How about your personal life? Have most recent conversations with your spouse, one of your children, friends, or other acquaintances gone well, or have you or the other person missed some cues that could have made a positive difference in the outcome of the conversation?

Even though there is a rapidly growing body of evidence supporting the importance of emotional intelligence (EQ), the emotional equivalent of IQ, many in our society remain emotionally illiterate.

Daniel Goleman, in his best-selling *Emotional Intelligence*, states:

> Much evidence testifies that people who are emotionally adept—who know and manage their own feelings well, and who read and deal effectively with other people's feelings—are at an advantage in any domain of life, whether romance and intimate relationships or picking up the unspoken rules that govern success in organizational politics. People with well-developed emotional skills are also more likely to be content and effective in their lives, mastering the habits of mind that foster their own productivity; people who cannot marshal some control over their emotional life fight inner battles that sabotage their ability for focused work and clear thought.

One emotionally intelligent leader who comes to mind is Max DePree, former chairman of the board of Herman Miller Furniture Company, member of *Fortune* magazine's Business Hall of Fame, and author of two incredible books, *Leadership Is an Art* and *Leadership Jazz*. DePree's effectiveness as a leader, manager, and executive can be traced directly to his emotional intelligence. Throughout his career, he was highly aware of his own personal strengths and weaknesses and worked hard to overcome the weaknesses while leveraging his strengths. But he was also keenly tuned in to all those around him—not just his executive colleagues and those who worked in or near the executive suites, but also factory floor workers, designers, and everyone else in the company.

DePree had an amazing knack of making everyone he encountered feel at ease and was a skillful relationship builder. He embodied a cornerstone requirement of meaningful leadership: an ability and willingness to reach out to others and engage them productively.

I have mentioned before that I am, by education, a civil engineer (a term my wife maintains is an oxymoron) and have spent nearly four decades working primarily with other engineers and scientists.

Engineers and scientists, collectively, have a reputation for being low on the interpersonal skill scale. Most people would simply roll their eyes back into their heads at the absurdity of those two broad professions having good people skills. Likewise, many who enter the ranks of management also have relatively poor people skills (what part of working with people, yet having poor people skills, makes sense?). I feel comfortable making such a statement because I have been there, done that, and suspect that many who worked in organizations I managed would agree I was not always the most emotionally intelligent leader around, particularly early in my management career. Leading and managing require that we learn how to put what might be natural (unproductive) tendencies aside, and develop ways to listen and empathize, skills that require we be plugged into our feelings—yes, you read that correctly, *our feelings*.

Leading and managing effectively with emotional intelligence require that we build a wide variety of ways to respond to our emotions, realizing that knee-jerk reactions are seldom the best way to build long-lasting, productive relationships with others. I wish I had a dollar for every manager I have heard say they really could not get into that "warm and fuzzy" relationship stuff.

Based on my own personal experience, I would have to say that most don't like dealing with the "soft stuff," or, for that matter, even talking about it, because it is the hardest thing they have to do! Fortunately, many have skillfully mastered their own emotions and have built impressive capabilities to productively connect with others. I firmly believe that everyone has the ability to do the same—but the real question is: "Do they have the desire?"

One very practical way to improve your emotional intelligence is to concentrate intently on what others say, and how they say it. Listen for tone, inflection and what is not said. Paying attention matters—you can learn much when you listen carefully.

Another way is to genuinely care about the needs of others; make their needs at least as important as your own. Emotionally intelligent people are not primarily focused on themselves.

Still another way to increase your emotional intelligence is to regularly reflect on your own personal strengths and weaknesses. Commit to working on improving your weaknesses until they become strengths and look for more frequent opportunities to leverage your strengths.

There are quite of few really good books on emotional intelligence available now. Reading several of them could help you build your emotional strength or awareness. Some of my favorites (in addition to ones referenced earlier in this section) are *Leadership and Self-Deception* by The Arbinger Institute; *The Servant* by James Hunter; *The Heart of Leadership* by Robert E. Staub; *Credibility* by James Kouzes and Barry Posner; and *Awakening the Leader Within* by Kevin Cashman.

Think about your own emotional intelligence. You may think you know yourself and discipline yourself effectively, and you may think you have good interpersonal skills (and you really might), but if you are really serious about knowing how good your EQ is, ask a wide range of other people what they think and how they feel. You might be surprised. By the way, if people feel threatened in any way about your inquiry, you will likely not get a true reading. You may actually have to arrange for some anonymous feedback.

Courageous leaders find 360-degree assessments an invaluable tool to get feedback from superiors, colleagues, direct reports, and customers/clients. I use such instruments heavily with executive coaching clients and the clients always uncover blind spots. I have personally had 360s done of my leadership capabilities and must admit that I had to muster a great deal of courage to face the music and learn from the feedback others provided me. However, had the experience not been an exceptional, eye-opening lesson about the value of seeing myself through the eyes of others, I would not—I could not—encourage others to do the same!

Would you really like to know what others think and feel about your interpersonal skills? Do you have the courage to ask the questions of yourself—and of others? With those thoughts in mind, are you doing anything to improve your EQ? I hope you are. You will be pleasantly surprised by the results of your efforts...and blessed with increased levels of influence.

Observation

13

'Unexpected' Acts of Kindness

Many well-known scholars, such as Peter Drucker, Warren Bennis, and John Kotter, have taught us that leadership is based on action, not position or rank. In a recent conversation with a friend and colleague, she used a term I had not heard before, and I immediately realized that it was a significant part of what it really means to be a leader (i.e., having heavy emphasis on action). The term she used was "acts of unexpected kindness."

While a popular bumper sticker that began showing up in the 1980s encourages "random acts of kindness," I somehow consider "unexpected acts" to be different. Both phrases suggest actions that directly and positively impact others, are at least somewhat unexpected by the recipient, and from which the doer is not looking for anything in return. But "unexpected kindness" implies a pattern of actions that are not just spur-of-the-moment reactions. In fact, such actions could well be thoughtfully planned in advance and repeated sufficiently often to have become habits.

The "acts" can be very small or substantial. For example, in today's society, the simple act of holding a door open for a perfect stranger is often quite unexpected, yet just a few years ago it was common, almost a given. The person doing the deed very likely does it regularly, almost without thinking. The person being assisted could be quite appreciative or totally oblivious to the kindness. Isn't it odd how we are often times conditioned not to expect a kindness? Regardless, unexpected acts of kindness to others are both thoughtful and generous!

An example of unexpected kindness can be seen in the acts of Tom White, a Boston contractor. White has, in a period that spans more than half a century, given away millions of dollars. While it is common for the wealthy to give large sums of money to support worthwhile causes, White's case is different. Often his donations escape the radar screens of the media that report on such things and his generosity pales in comparison to the levels of giving by the likes of Ted Turner and Bill Gates. But if White has his way, within the next few years he will essentially give away everything he has to help others. He has never sought recognition and does not expect any. He gives generously to causes (rather than institutions) he believes in his heart to be worthy.

Also, he did not wait until he was wealthy to begin giving generously; instead, from the time he had anything, he has selflessly used his resources to help others. Only recently has White been recognized for his generosity, and that happened without his prior knowledge or approval. Over the years, White has surely given from his excess, but within a few years he will have given away nearly all he has. In contrast to the giving of others, his generosity is truly extraordinary.

As leaders, we do not have to give away large sums of money, or maybe not even hold doors open for others. But we must be about serving others—often in ways that those around us are unaware of. To illustrate my point, I would ask that you consider the following questions:

- When was the last time you did something for someone with the intent that they not know you had assisted them?
- When was the last time you chose not to talk negatively about someone in her/his absence?
- When did you simply listen to another rather than providing him/her with your solution to their dilemma?

- When was the last time you chose not to control others for the sake of compliance—rather, you empowered them to be innovative and take sensible risks, and supported them?
- When was the last time you cared enough to find out the name of and say "thank you" to a store clerk, custodian, sanitation worker, etc.?
- When was the last time you chose to smile at someone who was obviously having a bad day and returning your smile was the last thing on his/her mind?

These unexpected acts should not be random; instead they should be habits we develop over time and perform regardless of where we are or whom we are with.

Are any of these acts significant? The answer is both "yes" and "no." They may not be significant based on the energy they require, but might be quite significant in terms of the impact they have on others. That nearly effortless smile could turn another's day around in a very positive way. The willing-ear-to-listen may be just what a burdened acquaintance needs to put an uncomfortable issue behind him. For all of us, many of the actions we perform will be visible, many will be recognized, and often they will be imitated, so the behavior we model is important. But as leaders, we must be doubly committed to those "unexpected acts of kindness" that could likely go unnoticed, if for no other reason than it is the right thing to do—and doing the right thing is a leadership responsibility.

Expected or unexpected, recognized or not, kindness to others yields its own reward. Our personal growth as leaders will be significantly enhanced when we act out of generosity rather than seeking recognition and credit for our actions. Over time, these acts of kindness and service to others become the fabric of who we are and what we do. Now is the time to start weaving!

Observation

14

Loyalty Is Earned Through Service

As I celebrated our country's anniversary on July 4, 2002, in the wake of the horrible events of September 11, 2001, I reflected on the notion of loyalty and the importance it plays in the quality of relationships of all kinds. Relationships between citizens and their country, between and among members of a community, between partners in business and life, between organizations and the constituents they serve, between friends and family members, between leaders and followers—all feed on a diet of loyalty.

Loyalty is simultaneously a simple and extremely complex concept. Regardless of the circumstances, loyalty can never be demanded. It can only be freely granted. No matter which type of relationship we examine, from the simplest one-on-one friendship to the more complex organizational partnerships that involve many people, unless an individual chooses to be loyal, it cannot be demanded of him.

Although loyalty is quite complex by nature, possibly the most meaningful way to look at it is to examine the relationship between leaders and followers. In his book *On Leadership*, John Gardner points out, "A loyal constituency is won when the people, either consciously or unconsciously, judge the leader to be capable of solving their problems and meeting their needs, when the leader is seen as symbolizing their norms, and when their image of the leader (whether or not it corresponds to reality) is congruent with their inner environment of myth and legend."

In interpreting Gardner's observations, Jim Kouzes and Barry Posner (*Credibility*) state, "Gardner does not mean that the leader will personally fix the problem," rather that, "people willingly follow the direction of someone who is attuned to their aims and aspirations, worries and fears, ideals and images." They further observe that followers "are ultimately the arbiters of the quality of leadership they receive" and that, "the people's choice is based not upon authority, but upon the leader's perceived capacity to serve a need."

Followers will be loyal when they see that their leaders are working tirelessly to serve the greater good, rather than serving personal interests. Loyalty is strongest when followers believe and observe that service to them is provided with credibility—that is, when they feel their leaders are both trustworthy and sincere. They will respond positively when they see honesty, integrity, courage, faithfulness, fairness from their leaders.

True loyalty seems to make sense only when the relationship works equally in both directions. Citizens' loyalty to their country is strongest when the values of the country and the actions of their leaders align with their own. The same is true in organizations—loyalty to an organizational leader is most true when the leader's values and vision support those held by followers. Loyalty between individuals prospers best when both parties in the relationship are dedicated to serving the other.

Loyalty is a powerful emotion, one that can even influence the personal decision to give what Lincoln referred to as the "full measure." Take, for example, the intense loyalty (and courage) of the firefighters and police officers who ignored personal danger while risking their lives to save others during the events of September 11. As we all painfully know, many died trying to save others. While dedicated service is provided to our communities all the time, the enormity of the events that day caused an outpouring of emotion toward those brave servants and their colleagues all over the country (and beyond) that has been truly remarkable. What an important lesson in leadership those brave and loyal public servants showed the world that day and the days that followed.

The events of September 11 forced us to rethink many of the issues in our daily lives, and to reconsider the valuable gift (leadership) given to us by the loyal people who serve us on a continuing basis, many of whom we might not even consider to be leaders. If I ever questioned the value of that reassessment exercise, the importance of doing so was driven home to me on July 4, 2002, during the annual running of the Peachtree Road Race in Atlanta. Among the 55,000 runners were three local firefighters, who chose to complete the 10K event dressed in full "turn-out" gear, including oxygen tanks, as a way of honoring their dead comrades. The response by the crowds lining the course and by our fellow runners was quite moving. Nearly everyone showed some form of loyalty or support to these public servants—some with loud cheers and applause, some with pats on the back, some running out onto the course to offer them a cold beer, some flashing "thumbs-up," some asking the firefighters to stop and pose for pictures with them, some with a simple but sincerely offered "thank you." The buoying force of support the firefighters experienced that day must surely have lightened the weight of their gear.

As leaders, we must work hard to earn the loyalty of others. We do so by the quality of our leadership, through the dedication of our personal *followership*, and by our commitment to serving those we lead by lightening their loads. All three ways of building loyalty are enhanced by the credibility of our actions, by mutual dedication to relationships based on trust, and by support of commonly held values. Our actions must always clearly demonstrate our loyalty to others and must always be worthy of the loyalty we hope others will show us. Are your actions worthy?

Observation

15

Vigilance and Balance Go Hand in Hand

On April 12, 1912, the Titanic launched from Southampton, England, on her maiden voyage with more than 2,000 passengers and crew on board, bound for New York City. We all know the story of the tragedy that befell the Titanic, the ship that some declared even God could not sink. But there are a few details about that ill-fated voyage that are not commonly known or talked about yet that are good lessons for us to consider as we reflect on our responsibilities as leaders.

Two days before the Titanic hit the iceberg that sent her to the bottom of the North Atlantic, two other ships sent messages about icebergs along her intended route of passage, but she continued on full steam ahead. On the very day of the collision, no less than six messages were received between 9 a.m. and 9 p.m., warning of a seventy-eight-mile long area filled with ice, yet the captain of the Titanic chose not to change course. Eventually, of course, a member of the crew spotted an iceberg (*the iceberg*) that the ship could not avoid. By then it was too late to change course, and, as we all know, the collision did occur.

Interestingly, even after the ship was damaged, most aboard seemed unwilling to get into the lifeboats either because they did not think the ship would sink, or if it did sink, there would surely be another ship nearby that would rescue them. The band played on deck, folks gathered earthly possessions, most chose not to put on life vests. The crews busied themselves getting the lifeboats ready, yet of the twenty lifeboats aboard, only three were filled to capacity. Six were only half filled and one was not used at all. In truth, the Titanic should have had forty lifeboats aboard to safely handle the passengers and crew, but the smaller number was chosen because the ship builders thought a full complement would make the deck look "too cluttered."

Irresponsible as some of these circumstances seem in retrospect, are we not equally cavalier or nearsighted about the organizations within which we lead? Isn't it strange how often we are so focused on certain issues that we totally ignore signs that could signal danger ahead? Isn't it odd how we do many things to protect an image? Isn't it unfortunate that we often do not have the right people working on the issues that really matter to our organization's effectiveness? Isn't it disheartening that we seriously underutilize the capacity we have by not having everyone working on the tasks that they do best? Isn't it sad that we go to the same few sterling performers with nearly every task rather than finding ways to enlist the talents, energy, and enthusiasm of our whole organization? There are many lessons we could learn.

As leaders, we always have the responsibility to look ahead, while at the same time paying attention to the present. As leaders, we must work to ensure we project a positive image, which is important, but never at the expense of substance. As leaders, we must dedicate our resources to and align all of the talents and interests of our colleagues with high-priority issues so we have the greatest possibility of achieving high levels of performance and effectiveness.

One of the most important roles of a leader is to match people to the tasks where they can make the greatest contributions. By thoughtfully distributing workload across the organization, we eliminate the risk of having a few "A-Team" members being so overloaded as to risk early burnout while others are underutilized and left disillusioned, feeling as though they are unable to make valuable contributions. All organizations are composed of a wide range of people with varying degrees of talent, motivation, and passion. As successful organizational and team leaders, we must find ways to identify both current strengths and opportunities for growth for everyone; while simultaneously promoting the expansion of their capabilities.

As leaders, we show how much we truly value others when we expect from them the very best they have to give. In short, we must lead by example, ensure that the highest priorities occupy our attention and energy, fully use all the resources at our disposal, and insist that substance rather than good appearance drives our actions.

Quality leadership must always precede (and complement) good management, otherwise we run the risk of busying ourselves and our organizations with arranging the deck chairs. Does it really matter that the chairs are straight if the ship is on the bottom?

Observation

16

Learning Is Fundamental to Leading

For much of my adult life, I have surrounded myself with people who thought like I did, believing that such reinforcement was the pathway to getting things done. What I failed to recognize was that when I distanced myself from those who processed information differently than I did, I denied myself the opportunity to see the world from someone else's perspective—in short, I missed the opportunity to grow and learn.

Fortunately, a wise and dear friend eventually convinced me how wrong-headed I was. The period that has followed has been truly enriching and enlightening, well beyond anything I could have dreamed. When I opened myself up to the ideas of others, I realized just how little I really knew. In the past dozen years or so, I have tried hard to embrace those who are different than me. Hard as I may try, though, I sometimes slip back into my old habits, finding comfort (though likely false comfort) in similarity. Thankfully, I have begun to recognize the symptoms—stale thinking!

My purpose for sharing this story is to encourage you to be open to all that is going on around you. Listen to people or groups who have ideas diametrically opposed to your own. You may hear a perspective you never considered before—one that could modify your thinking, your actions, and your feelings. It is also possible that the new perspective could galvanize the opinion you already have. Regardless, as leaders dedicated to growth, we afford ourselves the greatest opportunity to grow when we surround ourselves with the widest diversity of people we can find—then carefully listen to them. When we do, individually, organizationally, and as communities, we will grow in tolerance, understanding, and innovation.

Here is another related thought to consider—unless we accept and value diversity, we as individuals, we as organizations, and we as communities are doomed to mediocrity at best, or failure at worst. By embracing diversity we give ourselves the chance to soar.

Like it or not, we learn only through difference. Diversity, by definition, is about difference. Often, diversity is thought of only in terms of gender, race, and national origin. Diversity is clearly about such differences, but it is also about so much more, such as differences of opinion, ideas, ways of doing things, ways of thinking, etc. To many people, these differences can be threatening. One way to move from the negative to the positive view of differences, though, is through open dialogue. Dialogue is an exceptional tool that uses diversity for growth and understanding.

"Dialogue" has as its root the two Greek words *dia* and *logus*. Figuratively translated, these words mean, "This is my idea. What do you think of it?" Dialogue is a form of conversation that has as its motivation the processes of learning, understanding, and growing. It is all about hearing the differences and diversity of thought and using those differences to enhance, fine-tune, or change our current thinking. We can learn so much from others when we allow ourselves to be open to a diversity of thoughts, experiences, and feelings.

By contrast, those who are unwilling to open their hearts and minds to diversity are stuck with the opposite— similarity. How boring. The very best we get from similarity is confirmation of something we already know or reinforced agreement on how we already do things. The worst that can happen in such cases is prejudice.

Possibly the most important aspect of learning, however, is that it must be continuous. Peter Senge, in his seminal work *The Fifth Discipline*, emphatically states that lifelong learning is the foundation of personal mastery. Many individuals dedicate themselves to such learning because they understand the fundamental, critical role that personal growth plays in enriching both their effectiveness and their happiness. Leaders understand, if only intuitively, that learning must be an integral part of who they are and what they do.

While learning is accomplished through differences, we are exposed to those differences in a variety of ways, such as training courses/programs, on-the-job training and experience, reading, studying, listening to others, etc. All of these opportunities, however, fall into three basic forms—experience, reason, and belief—and each form is important.

Experience, it is often said, is the best teacher, and it may very well be. Some of the most important things we learn in life are those taught by skinned knees and bruised feelings. We tend to remember those hard-learned lessons a long time, sometimes a lifetime, because of the pain we experienced. But we can learn through positive experiences as well, even though they are not accompanied with the angst that burns indelibly into our memories. Learning through doing is a fundamental part of how most of us learn. Effective leaders look for learning opportunities in all of their life experiences, both positive ones and the not-so-positive.

Humans have a keen sense of reason that provides us with the capability to learn through our intellect and emotions. To varying degrees we each have the power to gather facts and process feelings from a variety of sources, analyze that information, and draw conclusions. Some of us are quite analytical and capable of complex problem-solving with tons of data. Others have high levels of emotional intelligence, are capable of sensing feelings, and know how to act in response to those feelings. Regardless, the ability to reason is a powerful, uniquely human gift that we must constantly exercise, sharpen, and build. The adage "use it or lose it" is pretty true. Effective leaders spend their lifetimes improving and learning.

The third and final way we learn is, for some, the most difficult way. Learning through trustfully believing what someone else says to us requires a leap of faith. Think briefly about the wide variety of people you know. Some are trusted confidants we feel quite comfortable believing (and learning from because of those beliefs). Others have a reputation for expertise on some topic(s), and we are confident that what we learn from them is authentic. Both of these examples of learning through belief are relatively clear-cut. But truth be told, there are some people out there who have not yet earned our trust, including those we are just getting to know, and those we know through direct personal experience who have not been forthright or authentic with us in the past.

Effective leaders work hard to develop trusting relationships with those around them. When they do, they can be confident they will be able to learn from others. Genuine servant-leaders also work diligently to ensure that they personally do everything in their power to be trustworthy, honest, open, and authentic so that others can learn from them.

The kind of lifelong learning that leaders must be willing to commit to, in order to truly make a difference in the lives they impact, requires all forms of learning. Which method of learning is the most difficult for you? Commit energy to that process, starting today.

Observation

17

Leadership Conditioning

About a dozen years ago, a colleague asked me to review an abstract for a paper that he planned to deliver at a national technical meeting of an organization to which we both belonged. The title of the paper (as best I recall) was "Dynamite, Barbed Wire, Air Conditioning, and Water Resources Management." I recall quite clearly that when I received the document and saw the title I thought my esteemed colleague had flipped out! How could this bizarre list have any commonality or relationship? But I had promised to review the abstract, and so I did.

Much to my surprise, my friend presented a rather compelling argument about how each of the first three terms in the title was in fact related to water resources management. As it turns out, the invention of dynamite, barbed wire, and air conditioning each contributed significantly to the need for managing water resources because each stimulated, in some way, the settlement of regions of the United States where water was scarce, access to water was controlled, weather was uncomfortable, or some combination of the three. Air conditioning made living in hot (and humid) regions an alternative for many, even though doing so stressed the water resource. Barbed wire has been used to fence in large tracts of land for grazing, often limiting access to water by other users. Dynamite has provided the means to move large volumes of soil and rock for construction of storage and

54

diversion projects. I was clearly intrigued by his thoughtful thesis; he had woven an interesting and complex argument.

Recalling this experience led me to think about all of the seemingly unrelated events of a typical week, even those that seem to be unrelated to our responsibilities as a leader. Those fast-paced, diverse events may actually begin to weave an interesting pattern, a pattern that represents a nearly nonstop leadership challenge for us.

Let's examine just a few. How often in any given week do we have the opportunity to set a good example for those around us? How many times a week do we encounter people who, by way of a simple greeting or a pleasant smile, we can acknowledge their existence, and thereby lift their spirits? How many young lives do we positively influence by showing them even a small amount of interest? How often could we be rightfully accused of acts of unexpected kindness to others? How many times a week have we allowed another driver to get in front of us in heavy traffic? How often have we accepted that challenging assignment at work, home, or church graciously, then given it our very best efforts? The list of similar questions could fill volumes.

I will not argue that such actions seem quite as disconnected as dynamite, barbed wire, air conditioning, and water resources management. The connection is all about exhibiting responsible leadership in everything we do, the attitude we develop and maintain, the interest we show in the welfare of others, and our dedication to serving them. I bet you never considered slowing down to allow a fellow motorist to merge in front of you as an act of leadership—but it is, and so is each of the other actions mentioned here.

Leadership is about who we are as a person and it comes alive when we choose to use our gifts to help those around us. Leadership is far more often exercised in the small things we do all the time than it is in larger, more visible events. The challenge we have each week as leaders is to practice our leadership skills by following through on the constant stream of small opportunities that fill our days. When we do so, we are conditioning ourselves to deal effectively with the greater challenges that present themselves less frequently. Athletes condition themselves regularly, in a variety of ways, so they are able to do their best in competition. Similarly, we must practice leadership in a variety of small ways on a regular basis so we, too, will be strong enough to effectively deal with tough challenges that would otherwise overwhelm us.

Observation

18

Constancy is Constant!

One of the most difficult responsibilities of a leader is being constant because (and this sounds trite) constancy is so constant! We must "be there" in both good times and in challenging times for our followers. Followers look to their leaders for unwavering support regardless of the situation. In many ways, the responsibilities of leadership in organizations are quite similar to those of parenthood in that we cannot choose when we must be a parent and when we can abdicate.

When couples decide to have a child, they sign on for twenty-plus years of teaching responsibility to, guiding, disciplining, and loving them—with no vacations. In much the same ways children learn and understand deep down inside that they are loved unconditionally, so, too, do followers.

In his marvelous book *Managing People Is Like Herding Cats*, Warren Bennis states, "People want a sense that their leader is on their side, that he or she will be constant." Constancy is a characteristic that followers soon begin to expect of their leaders, just like our children learn to know and expect that we will love them unconditionally.

How better to engender and sustain trusting relationships with followers (and our children) than to be dependable and reliable over and over again? I have always enjoyed the challenge of new assignments—doing the unusual—and have always attacked new situations with enthusiasm, energy, and zeal. If your experience has been similar to mine, you (and I) are able to sustain high levels of excitement, for a while. Eventually, however, the glitter starts to wear off. What used to be energizing starts to become mundane as routine sets in. Our attention to and enthusiasm for the activity starts to wane. When that happens, we run the serious risk of injuring our trustworthiness and hence threaten trusting relationships with followers, colleagues, family, and friends because we become careless in the details of what we are doing. We must be careful to stay the course.

But, be aware: Staying the course is hard work. It requires our full attention and can be very frustrating. The payoffs from our constancy, however, will be rewarded in many ways. Possibly the greatest of these is looking into the eyes and hearts of followers and knowing that they truly value their relationship with us and that our relationship is so strong that they never have to worry about whether we will do what we say we will do. Bennis also observed:

> If you are an effective leader, what you say is congruent with what you do, and that's congruent with what you feel, and that's congruent with what your vision is. People would much rather follow individuals they can count on, even when they disagree with their viewpoint, than people they agree with, but who shift positions frequently.

Let there be no doubt: Being a leader is a lifelong challenge, one that requires our full attention and energy. Are we up to the task? Consider the following questions— how we answer them is important.

- Do our followers know in their hearts that they can count on us?
- Do they sense that we have their best interests in mind at all times?

- Are we sufficiently dedicated to their service that we will not disappoint them by letting down our guard?
- Are we sufficiently dedicated to being leaders that even when we slip, stumble, or fall, we get up, dust ourselves off, and do what is needed to resume our leadership journey with renewed energy?

If we can honestly answer yes to each of these questions, we are well on our way to practicing constancy. If, however, we wince a bit (as I do) at one or more of these questions, there is no better time than now to choose to intensify our quest and practice being a leader. Lead on.

Observation

19

Tolerance Is an Important Part of Learning

According to Merriam Webster, *tolerance* is "the act of tolerating." *To tolerate* is to bear up under, to endure. So do the words *tolerance* and *tolerate* conjure up warm, positive feelings for you? If you are like me, both words generate somewhat negative reactions, mostly driven by the notion that if I *tolerate* a person or situation, I should immediately be canonized because of my martyrdom.

I have come to realize that I should have been more tolerant. To "bear up under," or to "endure" suggests that I have put a value judgment on whatever I am tolerating, yet when thinking about my responsibilities as a leader, I am forced to conclude that tolerating is far more than just enduring. If we value the people with whom we are interacting (and we should work hard to value everyone as a person), even if we disagree with their position, we can learn from them, though we may not accept their ideas. Whenever we confront something different from what we already know, we have the opportunity to learn, even if only to strengthen a belief we already have.

For example, Mary might support the notion that we should have daily staff meetings. I might feel that weekly or biweekly meetings are sufficient. When Mary's opinion is expressed, I can *tolerate* her position (with eyes rolling back into my head), or I can *tolerate* her position and attempt to glean important information from what she says.

In this example, her contention that daily staff meetings would be terrific might actually simply mean that she feels uninformed and the daily interactions would help resolve that issue. If I simply 'endure' what I think is a not-so-well-thought-out idea on her part, I might completely miss the quality information in Mary's message—"I need to feel more connected, more informed."

If, instead, I listen empathetically and participate in open dialogue with Mary, my true *tolerance* takes on a very different character. What might have been disinterested hearing becomes focused and empathetic listening. Rather than subconsciously filing Mary's message in the 'circular' file, I will be far more likely to seek to fully understand where she is coming from and respond accordingly. *Tolerating* her comment then becomes a leadership-centered attempt to learn, and, if possible, an attempt to serve her needs for both more information and more frequent information. I may still feel that daily staff meetings are inappropriate but could find ways to help Mary be better informed in ways that would meet her needs.

Isn't it intriguing how our frame of reference can significantly change the way we see the world? Remember, we see the world as "we are" not as "it is." We should spend a little more time each day looking for the good in people and situations, and for positive ways to 'tolerate' ideas different from our own. The results could be quite worthwhile. We might just find that we begin to think differently. In so doing, we may become more informed people and more effective leaders than we were before.

Observation

20

When the Going Gets Tough...

Recently, I was waiting for a delayed airplane in order to return home from a business trip. Sitting beside me in the gate area, in a powered wheel chair, was a man about my age. In addition to the obvious fact that he was unable to walk on his own, I could not help but notice that his right hand was completely missing and a significant portion of his left hand was missing, too. After a few minutes, Bill [as I will call him] and I struck up a conversation. In the next half-hour, I discovered that I was in the presence of a rather incredible man.

During the course of our conversation, I found myself asking Bill about his injuries, his military service experiences, and his current situation. Bill had served in Viet Nam, had been injured numerous times by gunfire and Claymore mine explosions, had been contaminated with Agent Orange, had experienced napalm, and had been shot more times than he could remember. His exposure to Agent Orange eventually led to his developing type-II diabetes, which in turn led to kidney failure and the need for a kidney transplant.

Bill told me about having recently seen *We Were Soldiers*, a movie reported to be one of the most realistic depictions of experiences by our military in Viet Nam, and being able to smell the napalm during scenes showing its use. He could remember being able to "see" the white streaks made by bullets cutting through the humid, jungle air. I expected at any moment to begin hearing venomous comments about his disabilities, chronic health issues, or his lot in life, but none came.

Bill related that not long after he returned to the United States, he learned that he had diabetes moments before he was about to make still another jump as a member of the 82nd Airborne with a full 110-pound complement of gear on his back. Just as he was about to jump, he passed out and fell out of the plane unconscious. Fortunately for Bill, his jumpmaster saw him fall and immediately dove out of the plane after him head-first, caught up with him, pulled his rip cord, and saved his life. Some time later, additional military service injuries cost him his hands and the ability to walk. Bill's candor and lack of anger at his fate struck me as amazing. If anyone had the right to feel sorry for himself, it was Bill. Courage, as we know, is acting in the face of fear or danger, one sign of a true leader. Bill truly was and is a courageous man.

I asked Bill what kind of work he does now and should not have been surprised at his reply, but I was. He has dedicated the rest of his life to helping others with injuries like his own by becoming a minister. We know that service to others is another one of the most important characteristics of a leader. Bill selected a vocation fully dedicated to serving those with whom he crosses paths.

The genuinely positive outlook that Bill has about life proved to me that he truly knows about several other fundamental concepts of leadership—specifically, taking responsibility for your life and, no matter what the circumstances, whenever you fall, getting up, dusting yourself off, and moving on. Even though his ability to get around is restricted to an electric-powered device, Bill is a rather remarkable example of proactively taking on life and gracefully moving through it. What an inspiration—what a leader!

Do we need to have suffered physical injury, contracted diseases unfairly, or taken on an occupation that is specifically dedicated to serving others to meet the tests of being a leader? The answer is obviously "no." But occasionally it is good for each of us to be graphically reminded of our responsibilities as leaders by meeting an extraordinary person such as Bill. My hope is this: that the next time I try to delay or ignore my leadership responsibilities because I am not feeling well, because I am not in the mood to be service-minded, or because I lack the courage to face a challenge head-on, I remember the half-hour I spent with Bill. He is, in my mind, courageous—a hero and servant, an inspiration, a leader in every sense of the word. What do you do when the going gets tough?

Observation

21

Love and Passion Drive True Leaders

Note: I think it is important to stress that I wrote this observation while listening to the one-year anniversary coverage of the September 11, 2001, tragedy. How very profound and appropriate. The actions of so many that day and in the days that followed should be remembered, memorialized, and held up as a litmus test for all sorts of exemplary bravery, service, and leadership.

Two emotions often associated with leadership are love and passion—love for others and passion for what we do. My friend Robert E. (Dusty) Staub (*The Heart of Leadership*) defines passion as the "strong desire to truly make a difference, make a contribution and to make something meaningful and worthy." Passion, in my view, is closely related to and connected with the love we need to have for those around us. Passion provides a real sense of zest for life and for what we do.

Defining love is a bit more difficult because the word is used (and misused) so often to describe so many emotions and conditions. In order that we might better understand what love means in the context of true leadership, I would like for you to consider the difference between selfish love and selfless love. Selfish love is the kind that expects something in return. Selfless love, by stark contrast, expects nothing in return, and is often called "unconditional love."

Leaders, true leaders, those who would sacrifice everything for those they lead, know and understand the real meaning of selfless love. They are the ones who serve for the sake of service. They are the ones who hold up and celebrate the accomplishments of others. They are the ones who, for the sake of honesty and integrity, are willing to hold themselves and others accountable, with appropriate consequences for their actions.

They are also the ones who are willing to give what Abraham Lincoln called the "full measure." Our country today is remembering the tragedies of a year ago, and, yes, celebrating the lives and heroism of the 3,025 people who lost their lives that day. Many of those who died did so almost by choice. They chose, because of their situation or circumstance, to put themselves in harm's way. I am obviously talking about the firefighters, police officers, EMTs, and others who choose to take risks daily in the service to others.

The events of September 11 brought out the very best in so many of those brave men and women. Some might argue that because these public servants get paid for what they do, they were simply doing their job. I would suggest that most of them were guided by a profound passion for and dedication to the service and well being of others, fueled by an extraordinary level of selfless love. But there were also many others at the World Trade Center, the Pentagon, and aboard United Flight 93 that crashed in Shanksville, Pennsylvania, who showed the very same kind of selfless love (and courage). Those ordinary citizens helped people around them (some of whom were perfect strangers) who were in need, and died doing so.

Others, the likes of Todd Beamer and his fellow passengers on United 93, realizing that unless they acted decisively they might be unwilling victims in an even greater tragedy, chose to give their full measure as well. Was it courage that caused them act? Yes. Was it a sense of service to others that caused them to ignore their own safety? Yes. Was that courage and sense of service fueled by a form of love that ignores self and expects nothing in return? I firmly believe it was.

Some other vivid examples of true leadership, guided by a high level of selfless love, can also be seen in the actions of several public figures who played key rolls in leading the rescue and cleanup efforts. Rudy Giuliani, for example (regardless of what you may think of his politics), visibly showed the depth of his love for the people of New York as the city dealt with the immediate aftermath of the tragedy. While he might have been expected to be out and about, consoling citizens, etc., the manner in which he did those things was the true difference. He went well beyond what anyone might have expected, showing a genuineness and level of caring that even the people of New York likely did not expect of their often fiery, passionate mayor.

George Pataki, the governor of New York, showed his own form of selfless love by quietly providing unconditional support to New York City's mayor, and doing so mostly behind the scenes. Selfish love might have caused Pataki to provide the same level of support, but that support would have been accompanied by much greater media exposure, thus, consciously or unconsciously, garnering more attention for himself. That did not happen.

We have already learned, and can continue to learn much more, about leadership from the events of September 11, 2001. Some of the most important lessons include the reality that there are far more leaders out there than we might expect (many of whom likely did not or still do not even consider themselves leaders). When duty calls, they are willing and able to serve, and that selfless love of others is an absolutely essential element of true leadership and an extraordinarily powerful motivating force to do good.

While the extremes represented by the actions of the loving people involved in the events being memorialized today vividly remind us of what real leaders "do" and who they "are," such things are not required. You see, many lead quietly, often unnoticed by the masses, while still others lead more visibly, but not for the purpose of recognition or reward. But regardless of the stage, each of these leads and their leadership is characterized by selfless (not selfish) love of others.

I would suggest that one important way we can personally show our gratitude to the heroes of this national tragedy for their sacrifice is by imitating the leadership lessons that so many have so profoundly modeled for us.

Observation

22

Treat Others with Dignity, Respect, Compassion, and Empathy

How much "greatness" are you willing to grant the person that you love most in this world? This question, posed by Roz and Ben Zander in their book *The Art of Possibility*, is likely to bring a smile to your face and warmth to your heart. For the time being, you can choose whatever definition you want for "greatness."

Granting greatness to someone we love is pretty simple most of the time. But if you are a parent and have a child who has chosen to stray, as much as you may love them, you may have difficulty granting them greatness, at least in the short term. If you are a manager and one of your trusted colleagues chooses to behave inappropriately, again, granting greatness may be difficult in the moment. So while we normally have a relatively easy time granting greatness to those we love or care deeply about, we must realize that doing so is not always easy; our love is often tested.

Here is a tougher follow-up question. How much greatness are you willing to grant to the person who is the biggest pain in your _____ (fill in whatever part of your anatomy you wish)? My guess is your response is probably significantly different. You might even ask, "Have you lost your mind? How could I possibly think about granting greatness to someone who causes me such pain, anguish, and frustration?"

If such thoughts were flowing through your mind,

I would simply ask you to consider the following: Am I "really" a leader (dedicated to developing, nourishing, and maintaining relationships with those I encounter, serving their needs, etc.), or am I a "conditional" leader, choosing to have relationships with only those with whom I am comfortable or who are star performers? The nature of your response is critical because, as principle-centered leaders, we are called to lead all those around us. "Conditional" leaders, as I have referred to them here, are probably not leaders at all. So, are you a "conditional leader" or a real one? Hold that thought.

To further explain what I mean by "granting greatness," let me summarize a conversation that occurred during a training session I was facilitating recently. One of the participants asked, hypothetically, how he, as a supervisor, could grant greatness to one of his direct reports if that person had missed three or four successive deadlines on assignments. I responded that it would be quite difficult for him to be granted greatness in that situation because of the numerous failures, but that greatness could be granted. We talked about the nature of the greatness that he as a supervisor should grant, but he still did not understand.

So instead of answering the executive's question directly, I asked if he was a parent. He had one son. "Would you be granting your son greatness if you allowed him to do something that violated agreed upon behaviors and norms with no accountability?" He paused only a moment then answered, "No, I guess I would be granting him true greatness only if I lovingly held him accountable for his actions (with appropriate consequences), and helped him learn from his mistakes." Bingo!

The same is true in the work environment. A leader who chooses not to hold a colleague accountable for inappropriate behavior or poor performance, but rather accepts that performance unchallenged, is, in fact, disrespecting the person rather than granting them greatness.

The poor performance or inappropriate behavior, in a real sense, is rewarded when proper accountability is ignored. Granting greatness after a series of failures is tough because doing so requires a leader to dedicate considerable energy to help turn the performance problem around. Most of the time, the damage can be repaired. The important issue in this example, however, is that the situation could have been prevented, or at least made less onerous, had the manager simply carried out his/her responsibilities from the outset. Ignoring the first infraction (and the opportunity to grant true greatness) started a pattern that would become more and more difficult to reverse. In relationships with peers, the exact same arguments are true. If we opt not to courageously deal with situations as they occur, our relationships are put in greater and greater jeopardy.

Granting greatness to another person is not about gratuitous smiles, pats on the back, and abdicating responsibility for holding ourselves and others accountable. Instead, the genuine granting of greatness is about treating others with dignity, respect, compassion, and empathy, balanced with courageously holding them accountable for their actions or inactions, even if the consequences seem unpleasant at the time. Granting greatness to those around us is so important that failure to do so can significantly impact our overall effectiveness, regardless of whether we are talking about relationships in organizations, families, teams, small groups, or one-on-one.

I am so convinced of this that I have chosen to develop *Armbruster's Axiom # 4*, which states: "We cannot reach our full potential until we are willing to grant greatness to everyone around us, including those who have vastly different ideas than our own." While we as leaders clearly have the responsibility of identifying problems and addressing their resolution, the more we choose to concentrate our energies on what and who is wrong for the purpose of casting blame, the less likely we are to grant greatness to the "offenders."

So I ask again, are you dedicated to true leadership characterized by courage, empathy, and service? If you understand in both your heart and your head that answering "yes" to this question is a requirement for effective leadership, you are already on your way to being a true leader. What remains is the often-difficult task of acting on our intentions.

Observation

23

Be Nice to Each Other

"Be nice to each other" could have been one of the life lessons that Robert Fulghum maintains we should have learned in kindergarten. While the message is quite simple, and one that even small children are capable of learning and doing, as adults we seem to struggle with the concept. The truth is it takes a great deal of energy, vigilance, and imagination to consistently be nice to others.

At work, colleagues might be late for meetings, might purposely hold back key information, or be thoughtless or inconsiderate of our time, our space, or our relationship. Similar lists could be made for our lives at home, with friends, at church, etc. Yet the power of respect and courtesy to those around us should never be underestimated. Even when people are in significant disagreement over facts, interests, positions, or expectations, it is the power of respect and courtesy to others that will bridge the gap, allow us to connect with each other, and move forward.

In some respects, a mindset of being "nice to each other" is a lot like the admonition to approach a dog that does not know us with our palms up. An upturned palm offered below a dog's face, for example, is rarely rebuffed. In fact, most dogs will welcome the petting that follows such a gentle approach. There are "people" equivalents to this palms-up approach as well. For example, we can approach another with a smile, a gentleness of voice, and a receptive ear. Leaders know that in order to influence others to follow them, they must make the person-to-person connection, and model behavior and expectations that promote dialogue and understanding.

Much of the time, being nice is not too difficult. But what about those times when our genuine attempts to engage another person are met with a sharp edge to his voice, a sarcastic tone to her comments, body language that screams defiance, or maybe dead silence at a time when silence is less than golden? Those times can be troublesome and challenging. With some effort on our part, however, we have a terrific opportunity to defuse such situations by fully using our self-awareness, consciousness, imagination, self-control, and, yes, our kindness.

Rather than allowing a curt response to our attempt to be 'nice' to provoke us to be uncharitable, we should give the other person the benefit of the doubt. Maybe they have just had a bad experience that has clouded their normal behavior. Maybe they are not feeling well. Maybe they never learned to control their behavior and you have the opportunity to be a shining example of civility for them. Regardless of the circumstances, your best efforts at being nice to others will nearly always be the best approach, even when those efforts are challenged.

Are there times when others should get the clear message that we are serious, disappointed, or angry? Obviously there are such times. But even when the situation calls for sternness, good leaders know that malice should not be part of the exchange.

Leadership is not about popularity—it is about getting results. However, getting results does not mean we can walk on the backs, reputations, work, or feelings of others. Leadership is grounded in community, and community is nurtured through high-quality relationships. Thus, as leaders, we must be ever vigilant about our feelings and demeanor.

The way we treat others determines how they will experience our genuineness, and, thus, our ability to lead. We should all make being "nice to each other" a part of who we are as leaders. The return on our investment in such efforts is high.

Observation

Trust and Be Trustworthy

How many people do you really trust? Why is it that we have such a hard time trusting one another? The fact is there is risk involved, to some degree, in every relationship. If you are very comfortable with a friend, relative, colleague, or spouse and that person has never given you reason to doubt his or her honesty, integrity, and intentions, the level of risk in the relationship is relatively low, so trust is usually high. If, by contrast, you have been betrayed or hurt in a relationship, the risk is much greater.

Risk is a lot like a chasm: the greater the risk, the deeper the chasm. If we encounter such a chasm while walking down our metaphorical road of life, we are impacted. How do we get to the other side? The solution is to build a bridge that will allow us to get past the barrier. Trust is the bridge that we need to build—but how do we do that?

Although we may not think about it in such terms, trust is built on a foundation of common expectation: There are no surprises. Stephen Covey (*The 7 Habits of Highly Effective People*) defines trust as being composed of two elements—character and competence. Another way to think of trust is that you know I will do what I say and will do so to the best of my ability. The inability of one person to depend on another to follow through on commitments is often the stumbling block to a productive relationship.

While there are some people who make promises that

they have no intention of keeping, they are usually pretty easy to spot. Even though these people may be obvious to us, building a trusting relationship with them cannot happen unless they begin to honor their word. But there are others who are not so easy to discern because their purpose, on the surface, appears genuine. Take, for example, the wide-eyed optimist who truly enjoys helping others. When someone asks him for assistance, the answer will likely be "yes." And when the next person asks, he, too, gets a "yes"—and on, and on, and on. Some might say the person whose intentions are good is just being overzealous. But making promises that we know have a very low probability of being kept is a basic, but real way, of breaching one's integrity. When a *promiser* does not deliver on her or his word, a small chink is made in that person's integrity armor. After a number of repeats of the same or similar situation, people begin to realize that the promises being made have little likelihood of being kept.

Each promise not kept is a withdrawal from what Covey and other authors call our "emotional bank account." Depending on the 'balance' in that account, the relationship may not be able to handle the withdrawal. Emotional bank accounts work the same as any other bank account. We make deposits by doing what we say we are going to do and doing it well. Over time, the balance builds. When we fail to do what we promise, there is a withdrawal of equity from our account in proportion to the damage done by not keeping our word. Just like with a regular bank account, when the balance dips into the 'red' there are serious consequences— trust is jeopardized and the relationship severely tarnished.

Let's look at some real-world events that could result in significant withdrawals from our emotional bank account. In the work environment, being overly protective of our 'turf' can cause stress in relationships with our colleagues, which in turn can cause hard feelings. Talking negatively about coworkers behind their backs can result in major withdrawals. And not honoring time and effort commitments can tarnish one's character and hence one's trustworthiness. In our personal lives, breaches of integrity cause equal and sometimes even greater pain because of the closeness in our relationships with family and friends.

In my experience, greater harm is usually done to a relationship when a promise is trivialized (and broken) than when a genuine effort is made to fulfill the promise, even if the effort falls short of expectation. I believe that most of us, most of the time, are willing to be generous when an honest effort is made. We tend not to be so forgiving when integrity is the issue.

Building trusting relationships takes time. Unfortunately, there are no special microwave ovens to help us quickly develop relationships with the speed that we warm a dinner roll. Quality relationships simply take time to develop—and they also require hard work on both sides. As leaders, we are each challenged every day to exercise our 'response-ability' on our side of the relationship equation. We do our part by living up to our promises as best we can. But we also have the opportunity and responsibility to influence trusting relationships in others by modeling the kind of behavior that clearly illustrates the value and power of trust. In the event that we fail on our side, even if that failure is unintentional, we must apologize sincerely and reinvigorate our efforts to ensure that we do not cause frustration, anger or pain again.

Leadership is an ever-present challenge, one that deserves our very best efforts.

Observation

25

Feed Your Spirit

The last of Stephen Covey's *7 Habits of Highly Effective People* is "Sharpen the saw," a metaphor encouraging each of us to take care of our physical, mental, social/emotional, and spiritual selves. These things should be a part of every leader's routine if he or she is to have the wherewithal to withstand the rigors and challenges of leadership.

Eating properly, exercising regularly, and getting sufficient rest and relaxation keep us physically healthy. Challenging our intellects—by reading the classics, doing crossword puzzles, playing complex games—will keep our mental capacities sharp, well beyond our working years. Filling our lives with family, friends, and colleagues provides the social stimulation and context we need to see beyond ourselves. Some of us need more social interaction than others, but all of us need some and it is healthy to ensure we nurture relationships of all kinds.

Feeding our spirit also requires attention. We can choose to nourish our souls by practicing our religion or by listening to classical music, by being inspired through beautiful art or beautiful sunsets, or by loving a child or serving our fellow man. Regardless of the way(s) we choose, let there be no doubt that nourishing our spirits is absolutely essential—we simply cannot function productively when our spirits are hungry. Most of these activities, while ultimately lifting our spirits, will simultaneously enrich the lives others. All force us to be in touch with our core and our ability to lead. Each puts energy back into our living and leading.

Because leadership is predominantly an emotional, heart-centered exercise, the notion of having a spiritual dimension and needing to nourish that part of ourselves goes right to the heart of our growth and effectiveness as leaders. Many refer to the spirit within us as our soul. Whether you buy into that term or not, it is critically important to understand there is "something" in us that drives our "being." During leadership training and executive coaching sessions, I often refer to that "something" as the fire in our gut that drives us to be who we are. For all of us, but particularly for those who feel burdened, unappreciated, overwhelmed, etc. with the normal demands of day-to-day leading, a healthy shot of exercise and nutrition for the spirit is in order. When we feed our spirits, we directly impact our ability to lead; in short, our "spirit" is at the "heart" of our leadership.

There are so many positive reasons to feed our spirit that it simply does not make sense to ignore that part of who we are. Ultimately, who we are drives what we do, and our actions determine the kind of leaders we are, since leadership is action, not position. A marathon runner cannot compete without proper nourishment, training, and rest. Likewise, we cannot be impactful leaders unless we dedicate time and energy to ensuring that our spirits are well fed, fit, and sufficiently rested to take on the next challenge. We must take seriously the nourishment of our spiritual dimension. We must nourish our souls to be whole.

What are the impacts of not caring for ourselves? If we choose not to take care of our bodies, we get sick, lack energy to aggressively live the life of a leader, and suffer the impacts of stress. Research now supports the 'use it or lose it' viewpoint, so we clearly cannot ignore our intellects. Not taking the time to work on relationships usually results in loneliness materializing in a variety of ways. But failing to nourish our spirits can have devastating effects.

I could not help but think just how severe it could get as I listened recently to graphic news reports of at least eight people being shot, apparently at random, by what was thought to be a lone gunman. There seemed to be no pattern to the gunman's selection of targets—they were old, young, African-American, white, Hispanic, women and men. The only victim still alive at this writing is a thirteen-year-old boy who was shot as he was walking into his school. Lee Bolman and Terry Deal, in their marvelous book *Leading with Soul*, warn, "Discase of the spirit exacts a high price. Spiritual bankruptcy ultimately leads to economic failure. The deeper cost is a world where everything has a function yet nothing has any meaning." They continue, "The symptoms of an undernourished soul appear in countless ways: violence, lethargy, alienation, alcoholism..."

Fortunately for our society, most people who choose to short-change the care of their spirit suffer only minor consequences. Even so, the results are still troubling and often debilitating—hopelessness in the old and young alike, disenfranchised employees, disintegrated families, corporate executives more attuned to their personal desires than to the organizational responsibilities to which they have been entrusted, and more. During his presidency, Jimmy Carter spoke from his heart about the concerns he had for our country suffering from what he described as a "spiritual malaise."

Bolman and Deal go on to say, "...we need a vision of leadership rooted in the enduring sense of human wisdom, courage, and compassion. We need a new generation of seekers...who have the courage to confront their own shadows and to embark upon a personal quest for spirit and heart, and who have the commitment to share their learning with others." Their observations are a compelling challenge to pick up the torch of leadership.

Being an effective leader requires a significant commitment by each of us to find and nourish his or her spiritual center. Effective leadership flourishes only when we consciously share deeply and selflessly of our spirit. The heart of leadership truly is in the heart of the leader. What are you doing, right now, to get more closely in touch with your spiritual center? What are you doing, right now, to share your spirit with others? If you are not satisfied with your answers, there is no time like the present to begin the journey. I look forward to seeing you along the way!

Observation

26

The "Soft Stuff" Is Really "The Hard Stuff"

In the introduction to his book, *The Servant Leader*, noted author and business consultant Jim Autry reports that he regularly hears three similar comments from clients when he talks with them about establishing a culture of servant-leadership in their organizations. "(1) Our organization is very different from other organizations, or (2) We feel that your ideas would take too much time, they're not efficient, or (3) What you teach is the soft side of management, and that just doesn't work very well in an organization like ours." How very profound! How very revealing such excuses are!

In my work as a consultant, I, too, have heard similar excuses for not teaching such concepts as servant-leadership, emotional intelligence, etc. I find so many organizations that avoid the 'soft' stuff like the plague. Why do so many find it so hard to implement such concepts on a day-to-day basis?

As obvious as it is, even though often ignored, most organizations have a common denominator—one that clearly makes them more similar than dissimilar—*people*. No matter what gender, color, race, or national origin, no matter where we work, what we do, or who we work with—all of us have wants, needs, aspirations. As Autry observes, "We have very similar hopes and fears, desires and ambitions. We love, we celebrate, we suffer loss, and we grieve." People are the common element in all organizations yet many don't want to be bothered learning about how to navigate the turbulence that can be associated with effectively interacting with others.

Rather than looking at our similarities and building relationships on that commonality, we often choose to concentrate on differences, particularly those that are annoying or irritating. Searching for people to blame or things that are wrong in an organization simply drains positive energy that could (and should) be applied to doing the business of the organization. In personal relationships, finger pointing and looking for what is wrong with others taints our interactions with them, often to the point of preventing us from seeing the good in them. So long as we concentrate on fixing what is wrong, we will never be able to maximize our personal effectiveness.

As leaders, at both the interpersonal and organizational levels, we have an obligation to help establish, nourish, and maintain an environment that promotes treating others with dignity, respect, and consideration. Those are the "soft" things that make up the realities of servant-leadership that we so often avoid because they are not hard like data, equations, etc. We each have the daily obligation to reach out to other people in need and to listen to them with empathy.

In case you have not yet discovered this fundamental truth—there is nothing easy about the "soft stuff." There is nothing easy about courageously modeling ethical behavior. There is nothing easy about serving others at the level we want to be served. There is nothing easy about treating everyone with the same level of honor and respect with which we expect to be treated. Leadership, particularly servant-leadership, might be the "soft stuff," but it is clearly not the easy stuff. Yet tackling the "soft stuff" is the single most important thing we do as leaders, regardless of the situation in which we lead.

I believe the main reason so many organizations have avoided promoting a truly service-oriented leadership culture is that they have yet to admit that the "soft stuff" is really the "hard stuff." While organizational cultures cannot be mandated, they do evolve in the direction that leaders lead. When everyone in an organization takes their leadership responsibility seriously, cultures can truly change and can become service-oriented.

Are you doing your part to help build a service-oriented leadership kind of culture in your part of the world?

Observation

27

Dialogue and a Cool Head

⟡

Have you ever noticed that in the midst of controversy, chaos, or unsettling circumstances, one person, fully in control of his or her emotions, can be the key factor in guiding others to a peaceful solution? If you have ever been in such a situation, you know the person with the power to influence others in such a positive way is a *leader* in every sense of the word, regardless of his or her job title. This is especially true when the leader is guided by a real sense of abundance, that marvelous characteristic of being able to see that there is plenty "out there" for everyone and thus win-win solutions are possible.

Often in the heat of conversation, a wide range of emotions is interjected and those emotional outbursts drive wedges between participants and an acceptable solution to the dilemma *du jour.* When that happens, if just one of the people involved remains cool—one who is dedicated both to solving the problem and to serving the members of the group—no matter how upset, loud, or angry the others become, an acceptable resolution can almost always be found.

Whenever more than one person is involved in a conversation, differences of opinion may occur. Those differences represent conflict—the spark that causes tempers to flare. Many people avoid conflict at all costs because they want to spare themselves involvement in those situations. But conflict does not have to spiral out of control. In fact, conflict addressed in a healthy manner usually results in a positive learning experience for all involved. As human beings, our capacity to learn from others is based fundamentally on the differences between what we know and what others know. Therefore, because conflict is based on differences, by inference conflict is an opportunity to learn. But for the learning experience to happen and to be positive, someone must guide the group through an exchange of ideas and feelings that clarifies everyone's understanding of the issues being discussed.

When there are differences of opinion, Peter Senge (*The Fifth Discipline*) encourages a form of communication called *dialogue*. True dialogue is conversation characterized by participants offering their opinions and feelings for others to hear and contemplate, and supplying clarification and comment—in a true sense of learning and understanding. Conflicts that might otherwise destructively unravel can evolve into healthy agreement when we strive to truly understand the perspectives of others and get clarification of the facts involved.

Dialogue in the presence of an "abundance mentality" is a particularly powerful catalyst to clarify understanding and develop consensus, even when only one person is so inclined at the outset of the exchange. When just one person chooses not to see issues as good or bad, right or wrong, and not see debates as battles to be won or lost, but genuinely strives to look for win-win solutions, the possibility of finding a solution acceptable to all is greatly enhanced. In their book, *Crucial Conversations*, Patterson, Grenny, McMillan, and Switzler refer to this mutual gathering of information as "filling the pool of shared meaning."

The power of a cool head guided by an "abundance mentality" can be critical, for example, in finding the solution to contentious issues spawned by office reorganizations.

Some of the issues I am referring to include rearranging office space and furniture, and realigning responsibilities. As we all know, for many folks, being assigned an office of a specific size, proximity to the chief executive, or having a window with a good view can be extremely emotional. When everyone insists on the importance of her or his personal needs and desires being met, solutions are slow in coming. Yet, just one person choosing to remain calm and act with abundance can defuse an otherwise volatile situation and move the group to sensible solutions. That one person (a real leader in every sense) is the one who listens to everyone's concerns and then helps to develop a wide range of options in an effort to find common ground and a solution that everyone can live with. They will sometimes choose to be the first to concede their own personal preferences as a way of stimulating a collaborative spirit among the group.

Conflicts that occur when responsibilities are realigned can be even more gut-wrenching and emotional. I have seen situations in which individuals who have had certain job responsibilities for many years (so long that they identify themselves with those responsibilities) find it difficult to accept the fact that they no longer have them. Some, consciously or unconsciously, will go so far as to interfere with the person newly assigned those responsibilities. When such role-boundary issues occur, resolution usually depends upon the manager in charge demonstrating real leadership savvy by remaining calm and focused, by being sensitive yet firm, by acting out of a true "abundance mentality" and by finding solutions that all are willing to accept. Such solutions might include reexamining role boundaries whenever possible; being creative in transitioning from existing responsibilities to new ones; and providing training to enhance new skill sets for those who will no longer be doing the tasks they are used to doing.

We each have many opportunities to lead others through difficult situations. Some of the most challenging of those circumstances will require even exceptional leaders to dig deep for strength, calm, and resolve. Remaining in control of our emotions is a powerful tool, particularly when everything around us is chaotic.

Observation

28

Listen, You Might Learn Something

The fifth of Stephen Covey's *7 Habits of Highly Effective People* is the habit of genuine, empathetic communication. As Covey presents it, "Seek first to understand before being understood." The term "seek," as used here, requires a profound sense of listening. The first time I read this statement it made perfect sense, but as I began to think about it, I wondered, "What if everyone waited for others to speak first? Wouldn't it be a quiet world?" It did not take too long, however, to stop worrying about the "silence thing" because there is nearly always someone willing to speak first. And, unfortunately, after some self-reflection, I had to admit that often I was one of those first-speakers.

The important part of Covey's message is that only when we listen first, and do so with empathy, will we have any chance of understanding the perspective, state of mind, or interests of the person with whom we are talking. Only after we have listened to their thoughts and feelings can we genuinely be in a position to share our thoughts in ways that are understandable by them. In reality, many of us frequently do an interesting and often frustrating dance around each other, speaking past each other, and interrupting, not processing, sensing, and reflecting—being far more interested in being heard and understood than seeking to understand the other's perspective.

Turn on nearly any of the national news broadcasts that have more than one person on screen at a time and you will clearly see what I mean. On any evening or most news shows, you can see five out of five people on camera at one time, all talking at once. No one there, or in the television audience, can possibly listen to that many voices at one time. As a result, little understanding or learning can occur. An underlying cause of our desire to be heard first, frankly, is pride. Pride tells us that because our opinion or idea is more accurate, more interesting, more useful, or more correct than those of others, it (or should I say "I") must be heard first.

Have you ever found yourself writing a clever mental script that you plan to "gift" another with as soon as they have the decency to shut up? I must admit I have done so on many occasions. Have you ever been mentally writing one of those scripts only to have the other person say something near the end of their comments that changed the meaning of what you thought they were saying—and in so doing rendered your beautifully prepared response worthless? Again, I am guilty as charged. By choosing not to listen attentively and empathetically, not working hard to understand, we waste time, both our own and that of the person with whom we are talking. In addition to wasting time, we are also being disrespectful.

As leaders, we have the responsibility to break this chain of not seeking to understand others by modeling effective listening skills for everyone around us. Albert Schweitzer commented, "Example is not the most important way of influencing others, it is the only way!" As leaders, we must work hard on our communications skills, particularly those involving listening. We can do so by regularly practicing being *first-listeners*.

As it happens, one of the most successful ways of getting others to listen to our point of view is not by speaking first but by listening first, giving them a chance to share what is on their mind and in their heart. When they see how we listen with interest and empathy, they are far more likely to do so themselves.

Unfortunately, a dose of humility is required to do this effectively, and being humble is hard work. A popular book published during the early days of the Total Quality Management era, *Quality is Free* (Phillip Crosby), advises that "you can pay no greater honor to someone than to actually 'hear' what they have to say." Such opportunities to honor others come frequently. We can show real leadership strength by taking advantage of those opportunities.

Observation

29

Practice What You Preach

⚬⚬⚬⚬⚬⚬

Several years ago, I heard an interesting story on National Public Radio. It seems that a dad arrived home to find his eight-year-old son sitting at the kitchen table, working on a poster for school. After the normal affectionate greetings, he asked his son if his mom had bought the poster board and markers for him. The boy said sheepishly, "She bought the poster paper."

"Where did you get the markers?" the dad continued.

"At school," answered the son, being guarded in his reply.

"Oh, I see," said the father. "Your teacher let you bring home the markers, right?"

"No, sir," replied the son, even more guarded in his answer than before.

"Are you telling, me, Son, that you brought these markers home from school without your teacher's permission?"

"Yes, sir," responded the boy, nearly positive that he was in some serious trouble.

With a great deal of indignation, the now-angry dad said to his already penitent son, "Don't you *ever* do that again. If you need markers for a school project, call me at work and I will bring them home from the office!"

The old adage about "practicing what you preach" comes to mind each time I reflect on the message of this story. The father clearly did not understand the concept.

Further, rather than taking the uncomfortable situation and turning it into a valuable learning opportunity for his son, he actually made the situation worse. In addition to not practicing what he preached (in reverse), the father provided a genuinely poor example for his son.

There are serious and far-reaching parallels being played out in our organizations and society each and every day. While borrowing markers from school is a petty crime, playing fast and loose with honesty in the corporate world and in government often results in the misuse and loss of huge sums of money that jeopardize the welfare and well being of hundreds of thousands of people. We hear about them in the news frequently. In the past several years, we have seen a number of giant multinational corporations and financial institutions brought to their knees because of the inappropriate actions of a few.

We hear and read more about corporate fraud today than ever before. This could be simply because we are so plugged into the news. But in *Managing People Is Like Herding Cats* (in a chapter provocatively entitled "Leadership Pornography and Optional Ethics"), Warren Bennis offers his assessment: "It is not simply that more of us are engaging in unethical behavior." He postulates that the real problem may be that, "more and more, we are unwilling or unable to identify or define what constitutes unethical behavior."

If the father in the story above is unable to discern that the solution he offers his son is unethical, is it not also likely that he would make similar judgments at work? Practicing what you preach, setting a good example, and living with integrity and honesty are not just good ideas. Each is an important part of what it takes to lead an ethical and moral life. While written long ago, the words of poet William Butler Yeats still ring true: "the core is not holding."

Our organizations, our society, and, indeed, we as individuals cannot allow an ethical deficit to ruin us. As

Bennis concludes, "Ethics and conscience aren't optional. They are the glue that binds society together—the quality in us that separates us from cannibals. Without conscience and ethics, talent and power amount to nothing."

Can ignoring the opportunity to teach a small child a lesson be an indicator of a deeper deficit in a person's character? I believe so. There are likely few responsibilities in our lives more important than teaching our children what is right and wrong, even when the object of the lesson is as inconsequential as a few felt-tipped markers. Yet if we are willing to ignore such critical opportunities with our children, there is every reason to suspect that other important opportunities will be ignored as well.

We show true leadership when we stand tall, avoid the temptation to act out of self-interest, do what we say we say we will do, and reach out to others. We are good role models when we practice what we preach, regardless of where we are, who we are with, what the situation—no matter the difficulty. We all face these challenges every day. What wonderful opportunities! How very fascinating that only when we act with humility, honesty, integrity, and service do we begin to discover our own greatness! What wonderful challenges!

Observation

30

Communicating Requires More Than Words

⟨⟩

Go into almost any organization, anywhere, and ask this question: What one single thing most needs improvement around here? The consensus reply is nearly always, "Better communications." Even in organizations that put heavy emphasis on communicating, the response is still nearly always the same. In an attempt to overcome this particular problem, many organizations have devoted a great deal of time, money, and energy to figuring out more ways and more efficient ways to share information with one another. In doing so, they have invested heavily in a variety of means to transmit enormous volumes of data, words, and images electronically and otherwise—yet the concerns remain why?

Most of us carry a major misconception that communication is primarily "message sending." In actuality, communication does not take place until someone receives the message and understands it as the sender intended. It is not an act, an episode, or an incident. Communication is a process that involves the active participation of both the communicator and the communicatee.

While we are flooded with newsletters, email, electronic bulletin boards, blogs, text messages, and managerial speeches today, our need for information remains unsatisfied because we, as individuals, are often not part of the loop. In other words, the communications have taken on the efficiency of a one-way street. But people resist being treated efficiently. Almost always, we prefer to be on a two-way pathway. Although often considered inefficient, the most genuine way to demonstrate that you care about others as human beings, as pointed out by Kouzes and Posner in their book, *The Leadership Challenge*, is to spend time with them. Face-to-face communicating is the richest form of communication because we can use all the resources of words, body language, voice, intonation, eye contact, etc. to deliver our ideas. While having face time may be inefficient, it is very meaningful.

As organizations, we should worry far less about communications and far more about *communicating*. Communicating should include as much direct face-to-face dialogue as possible. It should include frequent interactions from top to bottom (including conversations among managers and those two or three levels down in the organization), from bottom to top (with managers really listening, empathetically), and from side to side (without the normal restrictions imposed by organization charts). Because most of us are very busy, we must choose to schedule, rather than look for time for such important priorities. The impact on others is well worth the effort.

And a word about email: Email is a critically important tool and great for sending information, but as Jim Autry observes in his book *The Servant Leader*, "Email is generally lousy for communicating, so avoid hiding behind it. More good ideas, better understanding and more creativity come from personal contact than from blizzards of emails." Yet electronic communications are likely to increase in both frequency and scope. A word to the wise: Whenever possible, communicate face-to-face.

As for communicating with stakeholders, constituents, and others outside the organization, I believe the key to effectively communicating depends heavily on soliciting their feedback and on listening to them—particularly to the comments that are difficult to hear or difficult to accept. The criticism we least want to hear is that which we most need to hear. We must be courageous enough to see ourselves through the eyes of others.

As important as language is, communicating inside and outside of organizations depends on far more than just words. Some of the most significant communicating we do as leaders and managers, particularly if we take the notion of servant-leadership seriously, is through our actions. Our actions often speak far louder than our words. Given a little time, people can always tell when they are being coped with, manipulated, or outsmarted—so our behavior must be genuine in every way. What an incredible communications challenge for leader-managers! Are you up to it?

Observation

31

Be Aware of the Needs of Others

Awareness of and sensitivity to the needs and feelings of others are a constant responsibility for leaders. I was recently reminded of that obligation in the immediate aftermath of an injury that prevented me from doing some simple, routine, daily activities. The injury caused this very right-handed person to do virtually everything left-handed, including the signing of legal documents. I am so dependent on my right hand that using the other makes my brain hurt.

Be that as it may, I have been extremely grateful for all the kindnesses extended by family, friends, and perfect strangers. People reached out not only to help me physically, but also to support me emotionally. Their collective sensitivity and awareness of my infirmity has been sincerely appreciated. But in thinking about their thoughtfulness, I was forced to examine my own feelings and behavior toward others. Some of the questions I found important to ask myself recently should be asked far more often. These include:

- Have I been diligent in sensing the feelings of others?
- Have I reached out to help those with physical needs?
- Have I valued the suggestions of others?
- Have I looked for opportunities to lend an empathetic ear to another who needs to vent or unload?
- Have I been aware when my words and/or actions may have caused someone angst or pain?
- Have I apologized sincerely when my words or deeds

99

offended others?
- Has my behavior been a true expression of my deepest feelings?
- Have I been willing to be servant and debtor to those who depend on me?
- Have I allowed myself to be vulnerable?
- Have I shown genuine appreciation to those who have reached out physically and emotionally to me?

Often, we get so wrapped up in the hustle of our own circumstances that it is easy to forget that we are not the only ones on the planet. We are so busy just keeping up that we forget to look for opportunities to use the unique gifts that we have each been given to serve those around us. Still, when we are up to our earlobes in alligators, it is difficult to be aware of things beyond ourselves, yet those are the very moments when our true leadership mettle is exhibited.

I have often heard and read that it is easy to love those who love us. It is much more difficult to love those who are hurtful to us, or are disrespectful or oblivious to our feelings. Similarly, it is much easier to be kind, generous, and empathetic when one is on a roll and everything seems to be falling into place. But what is our behavior like when we are stressed or deeply in need of care ourselves? Such times are great opportunities to learn about the strength of our emotional intelligence and depth of our spirit—we can learn a lot about ourselves and our leadership capabilities if we just take some time to reflect.

There are also times when we need to be courageous and vulnerable enough to allow others to care for us. But even during those tough times, we can show our true selves through genuine appreciation to those who lend us a hand.

Throughout my life, I have been blessed with many wonderful people who have impacted my life so positively, including those who, even in their own times of need, never failed to uplift everyone around them, including me. I have been fortunate to learn many valuable lessons from them, and for those lessons I am deeply grateful. My gratitude for their generosity of deeds and spirit can be expressed best by a commitment to respond in kind. My sincerest wish is that I will have the wherewithal to do so. Each of us, as members of our individual families, workplaces, and extended communities, has that responsibility, too. Will we rise to the occasion and show the world that we are leaders in every sense of the word?

Regardless of our response to such a question in the past, we get exciting new opportunities to choose to act many times each day. How we respond is a direct reflection of our leadership. After all, our leadership is expressed most vividly through our doing.

Observation

32

The Legacy You Leave Is the Life You Lead

In Observation 10, I commented that every now and then, life throws us a curve ball. And I really believe that. But I never expected to have a second trick pitch thrown at me so soon after the first—yet it was, and I found it hard to both cope with and rationalize this second loss so soon after the first.

One of the genuine heroes in my life, my dad, graduated from his earthly life. Fortunately, I take a great deal of comfort in and am confident that he is now enjoying the rewards afforded to those who spend their life doing what is good and right. I am not sure my dad would be at ease being held up as an example of someone that was good. And I am not sure he ever really considered himself a leader, even though I have always felt he was. Over the past ten or fifteen years, he and I spent many hours discussing my work helping others to understand the challenges and rewards of leadership. I believe he finally knew and humbly accepted the fact that, at least from my perspective, he embodied everything we expect of real leaders.

So often we talk about the leadership requisites of service, courage, love, honesty, integrity, compassion, dedication, and hard work. I have been blessed to have a father who modeled each of those for me, and more. Let me explain.

Thinking about my dad makes it clear to me that, as a child, I always knew he was my father—not always my friend, but always my dad. I became particularly aware of the importance of this distinction when I became a father myself. The *key lesson* is: Leadership is not about popularity; it is about results and about doing what our responsibilities require.

After I became an adult, my dad was far more than just my father; he was a dear, dear friend as well. The *key lesson* here is: Leaders care about quality relationships and they never neglect opportunities to be friends. I was indeed fortunate to have the honor and joy of being both his son and his friend.

My dad's honesty and integrity actually cost him a couple of jobs during the years when I was growing up. While that sounds counterintuitive, it actually happened. Because he was unwilling to cut corners, improperly represent himself, his service, or product, or cave in to political pressure, he found himself on the outside looking in a few times. He was unwilling to compromise his value system so when he was unable to effect necessary changes in the organizations where he worked, he felt honor bound to leave and was courageous enough to do so. The *key lesson* there is: Principles are simply not compromised, even when doing so would make the path easier.

Important decisions that impact our self-esteem and keep us principle-centered often require courage. Dad always said, "You can go to hell for lying the same as you can for stealing." He also regularly reminded my brother, sister, and me that no matter what, "You have to be comfortable looking straight into the mirror each morning."

"Dedication" could easily have been his middle name. He was married to my mother for more than sixty-three years. Every day was not peaches and cream, but he was as dedicated to her as she was to him. The *key lesson* in that is: Even when the going is rough, we must stay the course.

My father was also a member of a fraternal order for

sixty years and donated many hours to that group's charitable works and the business of the organization. Dad was an active member of a men's organization within our church community dedicated to service and charitable projects for more than sixty-seven years, again donating many hours for the betterment of others less fortunate. The *key lesson*: There is significant value in serving others and giving of our time. Another *key lesson* is: We should work hard to have balance in our lives and to be involved in activities that cause us to reach beyond ourselves.

Even at the age of eighty-eight, my dad continued to work. If you asked him why, he'd quickly let you know that it was so he could remain active. He no longer did engineering jobs, his life's work—he was a bag boy for a local grocery store. Dad got genuine pleasure being out and about, meeting and greeting, gripping and grinning because it kept his body, mind, and spirit healthy. He put a smile on the faces of many people. *Key lesson*: The prescription to nourish all the parts of who we are does not have an expiration date.

I know my father would be quick to add that he had more than his share of what he called warts, those characteristics that are both visible and invisible reminders to others and ourselves that we are not perfect. And while he would be right, on the whole, his life represents strength, courage, respect, and devotion. He would also fearlessly and quickly say that his strength came from God.

In reflecting on the strength of my dad, it occurred to me that for most of his life, he was the mighty oak tree we were always able to lean on. Not a pine tree that bends, sways, and snaps in the wind, but an oak tree that stands strong and firm and dependable. But as we all know, even the mighty oak eventually surrenders to the grand plan of that same God who made him strong. Much like mighty oaks that eventually do topple, Dad was healthy, active, contributing, and vital right up to the end.

I would like to share what I believe to be an extremely important life lesson for all leaders. In the end, we will not be rewarded for the honors we have received, but rather for what we have given. Could there be a more compelling reason to lead? I think not.

So even in the midst of the sadness at his earthly passing, I am quite confident and, therefore, find great comfort in believing that when my dad arrived at the gates of heaven, the Lord said, "Come in, Frank, you have been a good and faithful servant. You have served many and you have given much." Will that same statement be possible for me, for you, when we depart? Only time will prove it can be so.

Observation

33

'Awe'some Example

From time to time, if you are an observant student of people, you will see actions from others that are incredible, to the point of being unbelievable. Recently, I was flipping through a magazine on a totally unrelated topic and saw a two-page advertisement that really caught my attention. The two pages were covered with a photograph showing a middle-aged, one-legged man on crutches, making his way down the street while six children were watching him with great interest. Such a scene might not seem too interesting—except the man was competing in a road race.

I prefer to think he was running a marathon with other competitors who were using two healthy legs. Whether the event was a 26.2-mile marathon or a five- or ten-kilometer road race makes no real difference. The impact on me was the same. The caption to the photograph said, "There are those who fall but get back up. Lose, but don't accept loss. And succeed because they will not fail. These people don't teach by words, they inspire by example." As it turns out, the advertisement was for *Sports Illustrated* and the headline of the ad, a play on the magazine's title—*Awe Illustrated*.

I have run in quite a few races over the years, including a handful of marathons. When I saw the picture, several thoughts raced across my consciousness. First, I have personally seen and competed with such talented athletes on quite a few occasions, in a variety of distances. Each and every time I was both awed and motivated by their courage and determination, driving forces that propelled them to do things physically that most would say could not be done. Yet they did. What an inspiration these brave people are to those around them! The second thought that came to mind is that we so often look for reasons we cannot do something, instead of looking for ways to do what we are capable of doing.

When we are tired, frustrated, disappointed, or indifferent, we can find a lot of excuses for not doing what we are all called to do—that is, to lead by example, with courage and determination. If we give in to the feelings that keep us on the sidelines, we will never experience the joy and happiness of leading up to our potential. Warren Bennis made a comment several years ago:

> No leader sets out to become a leader. People set out to live their lives, expressing themselves fully. When that expression is of value, they become leaders. So the point is not to become a leader. The point is to become yourself, to use your self completely—all your skills, gifts, and energies— in order to make your vision manifest. You must withhold nothing. You must, in sum, become the person you started out to be and enjoy the process of becoming.

Sometimes as leaders we are called to dig deeply into ourselves and look for skills, gifts, and energies that we might not even be aware we possess. My guess is that the one-legged man running with the aid of crutches likely did not set out to be an inspiration to others—but he has clearly been such for many. Through determination and hard work, he chose to perform in an arena where many would simply not have ventured. By doing so, though, other competitors will surely be encouraged to continue on when tired, knowing that their fellow athlete is giving his (or her) all. Are we choosing to use all of the capabilities we have in order to inspire by example? If not, now may be the time to resolve to do just that! Others will almost surely be motivated to do their best when they see us doing our best.

Observation

34

Leaders Must Love

In our society, there are far too few people who are willing to promote the philosophy and practices of social justice. Similarly, there are too few who are willing to step up to the leadership challenge. I happen to believe these two issues are highly interrelated!

What is the most important concept underlying both the philosophy and practice of social justice? In my rather simplistic view of the world, it is about consciously choosing to treat everyone with dignity and respect regardless of who they are or what they do. Do I have to like them? No. But all of my behavior toward them must respect their humanity.

While it is often hard to think about treating others with dignity and respect particularly when they are being hateful, we actually have total control over how we choose to respond toward them. Opting (or reacting) to treat others without dignity and respect implies that we choose to raise ourselves up as being more important than they. But real leaders do not see themselves as better than others. They know in their hearts that we are all created equal, and none are created more equal than others! Hold on to that notion for a moment.

One of our many constant leadership challenges is to love those around us. In working with a wide range of organizations and individuals both in my government career and now in my consulting practice, I find many people begin to squirm at that thought. You can see it in their eyes; you can see it on their faces—what does love have to do with leadership? Some, by contrast, seem to accept the notion without a problem; you can see that, too, often as a warm smile. I must admit I get almost fiendish pleasure watching the various reactions, especially from those who squirm!

For those of us who use English as our language, "love" almost always equates to a feeling. Unfortunately, in the case of this word, our language is a bit restrictive as compared to other, older languages, such as Greek. There are four different words in that ancient tongue that we have compressed into "love," but, sadly, much of the meaning has been lost. Jim Hunter, in his incredible book *The Servant*, says that

> ...one of those words is *eros*, which our English word 'erotic' is derived from, and it means feelings based upon sexual attraction, desire, and craving. Another Greek word for love, *storge'*, is affection especially between and toward family members... Another Greek word for love was *philos*, or brotherly or reciprocal love. The 'You do good by me and I'll do good by you' kind of conditional love. Philadelphia, the city of brotherly love, comes from this root word. Finally, the Greeks used the noun *agape'* and the corresponding verb *agapao'* to describe a more unconditional love rooted in behavior toward others without regard to their due. It is a love of deliberate choice.

Hunter continues, "When Jesus speaks of love in the New Testament the word *agape'* is used, a love of behavior and choice, not a love of feeling." The *agape'* kind of love is the love required of leaders.

So, leaders are challenged to love those around them,

110

and social justice requires us to treat other as equals. The common denominator here is rooted in the meaning of *agape'*. The fundamental elements of both leadership and social justice require that we choose to treat each other with dignity and respect regardless of our/their station in life.

The questions that we need to continually ask ourselves as we work to grow as leaders and as champions of social justice include:

- Am I doing everything in my power to treat others as equals?
- Am I looking out for the benefit of those who are being treated unfairly?
- Am I speaking up when I hear another being spoken of disrespectfully?
- Am I looking for opportunities to serve those below me in my organization as energetically as serving those above?
- Do I elevate the hopes, needs, and aspirations of others to the same level as my own?

We do have the opportunity to choose how we respond. We do have the choice about how we behave. Effective leaders make the very best of those opportunities.

Observation

35

Build Common Ground

Sometimes I think we forget that as human beings, we are whole. Being whole means a lot of different things. For example, it means that we have both a physical presence and a spiritual one. It means we are both emotional and intellectual beings. We have both a public side and a private one. The list of such *yin* and *yang* combinations is endless. My point is that each of us is a rather complicated creature. But the complication grows exponentially when we begin to assess the 'whole' of groups of people. There are some important implications to all of this when we, as leaders, operate in a sphere outside of ourselves. Let me explain.

For many years, I enjoyed (or at least thought I did) the comfort of being surrounded by those who had similar thoughts to my own. In fact, I worked hard, particularly in my work life, to avoid those who challenged my way of thinking, only to find out years later that those who challenged me were the ones I learned from most. As I began to see the 'error' of my ways, I started seeking out those who did think differently. While this was difficult at first, I began the hard work of building a deeper understanding of what it means to acknowledge and value differences between my thoughts and the thoughts of others.

Learning that lesson was not easy then and, frankly, I still struggle with it. But leaders must make every effort to grow in that understanding. In my work as a consultant,

I have tried to help individuals, teams, and organizations understand that it is only through differences, not similarity, that we learn. And for a long time, I have been reasonably secure in that advice.

But, recently, I began thinking a lot about and investigating the many dimensions of 'integrity.' Clearly, integrity is about doing what you say you will do. Yet integrity is far more than that. It is also about being whole, or integrated, as a human being. It was in that light that I began to explore the admonition to acknowledge and value differences and have come to realize that while difference is extremely important for our growth and learning, so is similarity, but for a different reason.

While acknowledging and valuing the difference between others and ourselves provides an opportunity for growth and enrichment, there must be some sort of foundation upon which those differences can be explored. If *difference* is the *yin*, then *similarity* must be the *yang*. Establishing at least a semblance of agreement on some level (on a thought, feeling, or action) provides the otherwise missing foundation for working through most types of differences or disagreements. My point here is that when people are at significant loggerheads with one another, with no basis for building understanding and trust, difference becomes a serious, negative barrier to any kind of positive relationship. If there is not some form of common ground, building productive levels of trust and understanding will be troublesome. In fact, even initiating conversation may be difficult.

Old-style position-based negotiation essentially assumes that there are differences between the parties involved (and those differences are sometimes galvanized from the outset, yielding unproductive results). But far more effective interest-based negotiation starts with an attempt to find common ground, territory that allows us to begin a productive interaction between those involved. Only through such positive dialogue are differences productively uncovered then explored, with the intended outcome being agreeable resolution.

No matter the setting, the people involved, or the situation, we as leaders have the difficult task of being catalysts, drawing people together in all sorts of interactions. We must be creative, sensible, courageous agents of reason, helping others and ourselves to develop trust through honest and productive dialogue focused on both differences and similarities. We must listen empathetically and speak courageously. Doing so effectively establishes wholeness in an important dimension of our role as leaders.

Observation

36

We Are All Born Leaders

When asked if leaders are "born" or "made," Peter Drucker (*The Leader of the Future*) responded, "...there may be born leaders, but there are far too few to depend on them. Leadership must be learned and can be learned." Similarly, Warren Blank (*The 9 Natural Laws of Leadership*) states, "I believe that every person has the capacity to lead. Some people may lead in the 'worldscape'; others may lead in small groups, still others in one-on-one interactions." Drucker and Blank both see leadership as a set of skills that can be learned, and I agree wholeheartedly with both of them. But from my perspective, I believe that *everyone* is born a leader. That may sound contradictory, but I do not really think it is.

Let's look at some of the most fundamental characteristics of being an effective leader, such as being an example for those around us, living a principle-centered life, working hard on developing and maintaining high-quality relationships, being honest, and living with integrity, among others. I believe we are all called to do those things and have the ability to do them with varying degrees of effort on our part. Another way of saying the same thing is that we are all born leaders; but some of us simply have to work harder to develop the gifts we are given at birth.

Clearly, some people have a much easier time accessing and developing their abilities to lead than others do. The fact that some find being a leader easier than others may be the very reason they are thought to be born leaders. Isn't it odd how we oftentimes fool ourselves into believing we are not leaders, simply because we cannot muster the courage to speak up? Isn't it troubling how we often find ourselves lagging back and letting others lead even when we see that they are not leading effectively? Isn't it interesting how our conditioned norms for our daily life contribute so significantly to our behavior? Isn't it curious how often we choose not to act on inner urgings with regard to our leadership abilities?

Al Capp, best known for his comic strip *Li'l Abner*, was a curious student of people and their behavior. One day he went to Grand Central Station in New York City, stood on a street corner, and attempted to engage passersby in conversation by congenially greeting them and asking if they had a moment to chat. He persisted for hours, only to discover folks seemed to be too busy, too afraid, or whatever. No one was willing to stop and talk with him. Being the curious sort that he was, Capp continued his vigil, but this time he periodically reached into his pocket and retrieved a quarter, then dropped the coin onto the sidewalk. Would it surprise you that all sorts of folks wanted to retrieve the money—either for him or for themselves?

Capp concluded that people seemed to be highly focused on and willing to act in those arenas where they are comfortable. In this case, talking to a stranger on the street in New York is not what the natives do, so they shied away from conversation, even when Capp tried to engage them. But when he included the inanimate coin in his experiment, some were willing to pick up the quarter and return it to him without conversation; still others grabbed it and ran away. Regardless, most people remained in their comfort zone, refusing to engage in conversation with him, whether they returned the dropped coin or ran off with it.

Isn't that same reality true with respect to leadership?

From birth, each of us has the capacity to be honest. But some find it hard to do in all situations; it takes them out of their comfort zone, so they opt out. Each of us is capable of living a life of integrity, but some of us do not have the courage to do what we say we will do, or we choose to make promises (because they sound good) even when we are certain we cannot live up to them. Each of us has the strength to live a principle-centered life; some choose not to exercise that strength because it is hard work.

All of us also have the ability to set a good example for others. Have you ever stopped to think about the impact you have on those around you? Listen carefully the next time you are around someone with whom you spend a great deal of time. My guess is that you will hear from them some of the phrases, expressions, etc. that are characteristic of you, ones that are your favorites, often unconscious favorites. We tend to imitate (or repeat) the words or actions of others, often without realizing we are doing so. A favorite expression used by a former colleague, "Well, there you go," is one I had never used until I heard her say it over and over in daily conversation. Soon I found myself saying the very same thing. We are told often that imitation is the highest form of flattery.

If we imitate small verbal expressions, it should be no surprise that we pick up and imitate other actions of those around us as well. But even more important is that others pick up words, actions, etc. from us. As leaders, we bear significant responsibility to ensure that our words and actions are worthy of being modeled. The things we say and do are relatively visible (audible) outward signs of who we are. Less obvious, but possibly more important to those around us, is how we feel about situations, people, etc. In their collective work *Leadership and Self-Deception*, The Arbinger Institute points out that we can fool folks around us—for a while. But eventually those around us will recognize our real internal compass. For example, if we simply tolerate others, we will eventually be discovered. If we always see ourselves as correct, our way of thinking will soon be recognized.

We are all born leaders. Whether we live our lives as significant, humble servant-leaders depends mostly on our willingness to take the gifts that we have from birth (even if they are only seeds of gifts) and develop them through hard work and discipline. Leading is not an easy way of life—that is why so many simply choose to take the easy route and not bother.

Leading is, however, rewarding beyond description, particularly when our leadership journey positively impacts the lives of those we encounter along the way. We get many chances each day to lead—or choose not to. Are you willing to accept the challenge to positively influence the lives of others?

Observation

37

Practice Leading Every Day

I have been intrigued over the years by the number of people, in a variety of vocations, who talk about "practicing" their professions. For example, attorneys practice law. Doctors make reference to practicing medicine. In fact, the "business" side of these two particular professions is called a "practice." I even find myself unconsciously talking about my consulting practice and my wife's accounting practice. Curiously, while there is much talk about *practicing* a profession, I am not sure I have ever heard anyone talk about practicing leadership! But practicing leadership is exactly what real leaders do—and they do it every day.

Leadership, in many ways, is an illusive vision that can only be approached. You see, leadership is the journey, not the destination. From my perspective, if we ever fool ourselves into believing that we have become the best leaders we are capable of being then we have stopped trying. How can we ever legitimately claim to do anything more than "practice" being leaders?

The following questions will hopefully provoke thought and cause some internal reflection about how well we are practicing to be leaders:

- What have I done today to serve those around me?
- Do I treat everyone I encounter with dignity and respect?
- Do I make their welfare my top priority?
- Do I seek input from others at work, home, etc., and

allow that input to impact my thinking, decisions, and feelings?

- What have I done today to promote a sense of hope in those around me?
- Do I listen empathically when others are speaking?
- Do I courageously face risky situations, such as sharing my feelings and seeking feedback?
- Do I genuinely assess whether my own personal core values are aligned with those of the organization within which I work?
- Do I consistently hold myself and others accountable?

I have a theory that no matter how much energy we put into these and similar efforts, even when we do our best (whatever 'best' is at that time), there is always room for improvement. An interesting corollary to this theory is that those who work the hardest at being really good leaders are the same ones who work hardest to figure out ways to be even better leaders! For more than two decades as a manager, I found the very same thing to be true of our best performers in all kinds of positions—they were the ones who consistently wanted to find ways to contribute even more than they were already contributing.

In his now famous book, *Everything I Ever Needed to Know in Life I Learned in Kindergarten*, Robert Fulghum tells a story about personally meeting Mother Theresa of Calcutta. Fulghum was present at the ceremony in Stockholm when Mother Theresa was awarded the Nobel Prize for Peace. As I read his story, I tried to put myself in his place, and in doing so I found myself reflecting about my own personal responsibilities as a leader. Like Fulghum, when I compare myself to Mother Theresa, I feel woefully inadequate—not just in a different league, on an entirely different planet! Yet from reading the story, it became quite apparent that Mother Theresa did not see herself as anything special, despite the accolades heaped upon her. She preferred to see the work being done by her and her community as being quite ordinary, but done with great love and compassion. Think about it. They worked with what she called the poorest of the poor. How could their work be done in any other way?

The challenges we face each day as leaders may not be as daunting as those faced by people working with the poor of Calcutta, or those with AIDS, or those in physical, emotional, or financial distress, but meeting our challenge requires courageous and effective conditioning, similar to the conditioning done by athletes. Conditioning ourselves to be ready to face difficult leadership challenges requires that we regularly practice being leaders. The more we practice, the better we get. The more we practice, the more effective we become. The more we practice, the more others willingly choose to follow. The more we practice, the more we learn how better to serve.

Leadership is an upwardly expanding spiral of learning, committing, and doing. Each of us must take stock of where we are on the spiral. What do we need to do to continue that upward journey?

Just one more thought: The next time we find ourselves drifting into even a small amount of self-pity concerning our ability to really make a difference, we would do well to reflect on that tiny little woman in India who left her comfortable job as a schoolteacher in order to help those in the most dire of circumstances. Yes, we can make true differences as leaders when we are willing to practice, practice, practice.

Observation

38

Focus and Discipline Will Help Us Get to the Winners' Circle

⎯⎯⎯ ◦≪≫◦ ⎯⎯⎯

What separates highly effective leaders from those who are not so effective? The answer may lie in our internal compass and our focus on doing what is right, despite distractions, interruptions, or other complications. This particular insight came to me, as odd as it may seem, while watching the Kentucky Derby!

Owners, trainers, and jockeys alike work hard to ensure that their horses remain as focused on running their own race as possible. Thoroughbreds are rather high-spirited and are easily distracted. But these incredible animals are filled with a great deal of ability and inner drive to run. So, one of the biggest challenges jockeys face is keeping their horses focused on the race. In addition, the jockeys must pace the horses in such a way that they run within their capabilities so they have sufficient energy near the end of the race, to make their final run to finish line.

One important way they keep their horses focused is with blinders—minimizing the visual distractions caused by other horses and jockeys nearby. Pacing is far more difficult to regulate. Each jockey must know both the strengths and weaknesses of her/his mount, taking advantage of the strengths and minimizing the weaknesses. Highly spirited horses, for example, leave the starting gate at sprint speed and if not disciplined in some way, will expend most of their energy long before the final turn. Knowing that, the jockey holds the horse back a bit at the beginning then lets the horse run near the end. Each horse has its own race capabilities and must be ridden to take full advantage of those capabilities. For the jockey to ride the race in any other way would jeopardize any chance for a win.

As leaders, we, too, must be highly focused and disciplined, regardless of the distractions. We must recognize our own personal strengths and weaknesses, taking advantage of the strengths and working hard to improve where we are not so strong. Unlike racing thoroughbreds, we do not wear leather barriers to physically prevent us from being distracted. In fact, as leaders we must be fully aware of the wide range of people and situations around us. We must depend on other sorts of blinders if we are to remain dedicated to our responsibility as leaders. For example, intense focus on the needs and feelings of the people around us will ensure that we are dedicated to them no matter what forces might try to pull us away.

Pacing (discipline, if you prefer) is another critical driver for us to master as we strive to be effective leaders. Scott Peck, in *The Road Less Traveled*, points out that personal discipline requires that we be willing to delay gratification, take full responsibility for ourselves, be truthful in all things, and remain balanced. This sage advice constitutes the foundation for personal pacing of ourselves. Many leaders become so engrossed in the activity of their calling that they forget to take care of themselves. Taking time to relax, reflect, and renew is an important ingredient for each of us if we are to remain in the leadership race for the long term. Feverish bursts of leadership excitement and action are quite helpful in keeping us invigorated and connected. But if we fail to operate at a pace that we can reasonably handle, then we run the risk of burnout, illness, and collapse.

Occasionally a horse will choose not to run energetically so jockeys must 'encourage' them to do so. We should be wary of similar tendencies in ourselves and be willing to do what is necessary to self-motivate.

I think it is important to note that even the most talented racehorses cannot run at full speed all the time, including the ones that make it to the winners' circle, and even the most energetic and talented thoroughbreds cannot run in every race. Likewise, if we intend to be effective leaders over the long term (and arrive at our own personal winners' circle), we would do well to take lessons from these four-legged wonders and run our own race—stay focused, operate within our capability, train regularly, and get plenty of rest and relaxation. The best leaders understand that they do not have to be in the lead all the time, so they give others the chance to learn and grow by passing the baton to them from time to time. Doing so not only gives leaders a bit of a breather, it also helps develop the talents of aspiring leaders—a win-win situation for all.

Staying focused on our leadership responsibilities and being highly disciplined will add to our effectiveness, regardless of the situation.

Observation

39

Courageously Challenge and Push Back

Several years ago, General Colin Powell, former chairman of the Joint Chiefs of Staff and later secretary of state, gave a talk as part of his Outreach to America program. In his presentation, Powell articulated eighteen leadership lessons. One of those lessons, Lesson 4, caught my attention: "Don't be afraid to challenge the pros, even in their own backyard." Learn from the pros, observe them, seek them out as mentor and partners. But remember that even the pros may have leveled out in terms of their learning and skills.

Sometimes even the pros can become complacent and lazy. Leadership does not emerge from blind obedience to anyone. Xerox's Barry Rand was right on target when he warned his people that if you "have a yes-man working for you, one of you is redundant. Good leadership encourages everyone's evolution."

Powell was right on target, too. So often we tend to abdicate our leadership responsibilities, particularly in the presence of someone higher up in our organization or someone more technically competent than we. We probably do so because we assume that since we are lower in the organization or less experienced, our ideas may not be as good as those of someone higher. But little could be further from the truth. Position in an organization does not guarantee the best or most effective ideas. Position in an organization, in fact, does not guarantee that the senior-most people are even leaders!

Effective leaders, no matter where they sit, are successful, in large part, because they listen and learn from everyone around them. Because no two of us are exactly alike, we each have the opportunity to add richness to any situation, if only by asking a question, challenging a statement, or responsibly holding others accountable. Leaders who understand these concepts actually invite differing positions and are comfortable entertaining such opinions.

Unfortunately, some managers who think they are leaders will say the right words but, when challenged, will retaliate and send messages that are neither positive nor useful. The first negative message they send is that they lack integrity (they invite differing opinions but when such opinions are offered, the messenger becomes a victim). The second message sent to the dissenter is that his/her opinion does not really matter. The third message is that over the long term, people in lower positions in the organization should keep their opinions to themselves. All three messages are counterproductive at best, but destructive at worst.

Let's examine whether we might be guilty of sending such messages.

- Do I get defensive when others disagree with me?
- Do I lean toward anger when I do not get my way?
- Are my actions contrary to my words?
- Do I listen to others only when they are higher in the organization than I am?

An affirmative response to any these questions is almost surely a problem. Tendencies that would cause us to respond "yes" are rooted in pride, arrogance, and a lack of integrity — three characteristics diametrically opposed to real leadership.

By contrast, if we courageously accept (or invite) feedback from others, even when our opinion is contradicted, we learn valuable lessons. If we keep our cool when things do not go our way, we show others that we respect them as fellow human beings and we respect their opinions as well.

When our actions are fully aligned with our words, others will know we are people of integrity and trust us. When we value the opinions of others regardless of their position, we let them know concretely that this is a learning organization and that learning takes many forms and flows in all directions. Further, we say loud and clear, by our actions, that good ideas can come from anyone, and we want to hear them.

While the pros (as Powell refers to them) might have the most experience, maybe even be the brightest around, they are not the sole source of valuable information. We clearly need to take advantage of what these highly experienced folks have to offer, but if we act only on their ideas or insights, we are likely to be married to the past, or at best be encouraged to promote only the present.

Real growth occurs when we take advantage of historical lessons, critically define and shape the present, challenge the pros, and have the courage to step beyond our experience and pursue our vision of the future.

Observation

40

Care Enough to Bother

In the New Testament of the Bible, Mark (Chapter 2, v 1-12) relates a wonderful story about a group of friends who, in a desperate effort to help a friend who is crippled, decide to try to get him close to Jesus so that he might be cured. Unfortunately, they were prevented from doing so by a large crowd that had gathered. Not to be deterred, they decided to climb up onto the roof of the house where Jesus was visiting, cut a hole into the roof, and lower their friend on a pallet into the room where Jesus was teaching.

I have always found this story quite interesting for several reasons, but there is one that I would like to concentrate on here. How many of us are sufficiently dedicated to overcoming enormous obstacles in order to help others? How many friends would bother? Regardless of our religious persuasion, there are terrific leadership lessons we can learn from stories like this one about people who care enough about someone else to be bothered.

To illustrate my point, I would pose just one simple question: How often have we allowed ourselves to be bothered by someone who has come to us with a concern during a busy day and have cared enough to give her or him our full attention for a few minutes? The answer to this question speaks volumes about our dedication to leadership.

Clearly our efforts do not need to be as dramatic as those in the story of the paralyzed man being lowered through the roof (although that level of effort might sometimes be required). However, our willingness to be bothered must clearly rise to such a level of caring that those around us will seek us out, knowing that we care sufficiently about them to make the time to be fully present to them. Being fully present to others is a concept steeped in our obligation to give our full and undivided attention, listen empathetically, and treat people with love (i.e., at least the *agape'* form of love).

Colin Powell once commented that when the troops stop coming to you with their concerns (he specifically did not say to "solve their problems"), you no longer lead. Family, friends, colleagues, and others who look to us are often not looking for someone to solve their problems nearly as often as they simply need someone to hear them out. The simple vocalization of their concern, angst, etc. to another human being who chooses to be concerned and listen is all they may need in the way of help. On those occasions, we need to listen with both the ears in our head as well as those in our heart. We cannot allow ourselves to be distracted, disinterested, or otherwise occupied.

There will be times when we are juggling so many issues that we cannot stop in that moment to add even one more to the mix, but most people understand and are willing to schedule a time when we can give them our full attention. Oftentimes when we are approached, the person who needs our attention will ask, "Can I bother you?" or "Is this a bad time?" or "I need a few minutes of your time...do you have time now?" or some variation on those themes. The point is that people generally know that the moment they come to us might not be a great time, and they are willing to wait for one that is. Most would rather have a few minutes of quality time with us later than to talk now, knowing or suspecting that we have our attention elsewhere.

During my lifetime, I have tried hard to be present to others in need when they approached, and sometimes was able to do so with undivided attention. However, far too often, in an effort to look good or make a good impression, I have been disingenuous in my presence with them. Characteristic activities for me included (but were not limited to) fiddling with papers on my desk, looking at my watch, glancing at my computer monitor, or, possibly worst of all, appearing to be attentive, but mentally, emotionally, and spiritually being a thousand miles away.

Our ability to lead is directly linked to our willingness to enter into relationships with others, which in turn is directly linked to our willingness to be bothered by them. When family, friends, and colleagues both know in their heads and feel in their hearts that we care, we will have proven our love for them.

The friends of the paralytic man in Saint Mark's gospel showed us how to lead by lifting him up and lowering him into the house. We do the same thing each time we give our full and undivided attention and energy to others. Leading effectively means that we are willing to be bothered by those who need our time, our presence, our attention, our ears, our hearts. We must graciously allow ourselves to be bothered and in so doing lift them up.

Observation

41

Humility Is the Soul of Leadership

In my consulting work, I frequently ask a question that I first saw posed by Roz and Ben Zander (*The Art of Possibility*): "How much greatness are you willing to grant those around you?" (I introduced this question in Observation 22.) I usually suggest to people that they should use whatever definition of greatness they find most meaningful. In return, I am often asked what my definition of 'greatness' is. Most of the time my responses focus on some aspects of serving or respecting others, *agape'*, etc. I usually add that granting greatness to another person is not about gratuitous smiles, pats on the back, and abdicating responsibility for holding ourselves and others accountable. Instead, the genuine granting of greatness is about treating others with dignity, respect, compassion, and empathy balanced with courageously holding them accountable for their actions or inactions, even if the consequences seem unpleasant at the time.

Recently, however, in a conversation with a friend, I began to see a new dimension of granting greatness to others that I had never considered—one that provides a much richer, more significant insight than I had before. This new understanding came quickly into focus as I listened intently to my friend speak about the essence of greatness. At the very moment I heard him say, "Humility is the soul of greatness," I realized that the most fundamental meaning of granting greatness to another, regardless of who or where they are or what they have done, comes to life when we humble ourselves before them. What a challenging thought! What a challenging call to action!

I have said many times that the responsibilities of being a leader in the purest form include being a role model, serving the legitimate needs others, and being respectful of everyone we encounter. But in living out these responsibilities, there is an interesting paradox that complicates our desire to be truly effective leaders. Charles Manz, in his very popular book *The Leadership Wisdom of Jesus*, says that our own greatness

> ...comes more from avoiding [greatness rather] than from seeking it. Or maybe more accurately, the seeds of greatness derive from humility and service. Don't seek honor. Rather, let it seek you in its own way and when the time is right. Don't even think about it. Go about your business pursuing constructive work and focus on honoring and recognizing the contributions of others rather than your own. If you do this sincerely, your efforts will often receive the recognition they deserve, and more, as long as you don't seek and expect it.

What does this mean in the context of treating others with dignity, respect, compassion, and empathy, balanced with courageously holding them accountable for their actions or inactions, as mentioned earlier? Simply this: When we act with true humility, we act without arrogance or excessive pride in ourselves or in our own achievements. In essence, when we are genuinely humble, we will act with a true sense of submission to others. By contrast, when we allow ourselves to get caught up in our own importance, we quickly slip into vanity—and vanity clouds our ability to act effectively. Kouzes and Posner (*Credibility*) point out that the only true antidote to vanity is humility.

Much of the time we will find it relatively simple to grant greatness to those we love (because they are easy to be with), but much more difficult to do the same for those who are personal challenges (they not only get on our nerves, they seem to know the location of our very last nerve). In truth, however, the opposite case could be made, particularly with those with whom we are close. With them, we may very well find that issues surrounding pride are difficult to set aside. Sibling rivalries and professional jealousies, for example, can rear their heads when we least expect and prevent us from granting greatness.

In other situations, the need to appear strong and invincible in the eyes of a loved one or colleague may cause us to leave humility in the wings as well. But if we act courageously and allow ourselves to be vulnerable, we will discover that humility becomes a growing part of who we are and what we do. The logical result of increased humility is a reduction in excessive pride, vanity, and arrogance, all of which hold us back.

In his book *The Heart of Leadership*, Dusty Staub eloquently describes how and why competence, integrity, intimacy, and passion are the four chambers of the leadership heart. He also describes convincingly (in *The 7 Acts of Courage*) the role and importance of courage in exercising these four leadership components. If these fundamental elements define the heart of leadership (and I firmly believe they do), humility must be the *soul* of leadership greatness.

Nathaniel Hawthorne once wrote, "Happiness is as a butterfly which, when pursued, is always beyond our grasp, but which, if you will sit down quietly, may alight upon you." Precisely the same comment could be made of greatness: "The true path to great leadership is to be humble and look for the greatness in others" (*The Leadership Wisdom of Jesus*).

Are we on a path toward true greatness? Rather than looking at our stature, honors received, financial success, etc., we might want to assess our willingness to be humble in the presence of everyone. Humility is, after all, the soul of greatness, so focusing on it will keep us moving in the right direction, allowing us to positively impact the lives of others, regardless of the circumstances.

Knowing now that doing so requires humility, just how much greatness are you willing to grant those you encounter?

Observation

42

The Yin and Yang of Leadership and Followership

Every now and then, a photograph appears on a magazine cover, in the newspaper, or elsewhere that not only catches our attention but also becomes indelibly recorded in our memory. For example, in 1985, the cover of *National Geographic* magazine featured the face of a teenage Afghani girl, a war refugee, with penetrating gray eyes. The young woman's face was so engaging and evoked such deep emotion that *National Geographic* went back to Afghanistan more than twenty-five years later to find her as an adult, in the aftermath of still another war.

Nearly everyone has a clear memory of the famous photo of a GI and a young woman kissing during the celebrations in New York as our troops returned home from World War II. And who could forget the picture of the New York City firefighters raising the American flag over the debris pile at the World Trade Center or the one of U.S. Marines raising the flag on Iwo Jima? Images such as these impact us deeply in so many ways.

I came across another such photograph recently that left a significant impression on me. This picture might never become an icon in the minds of others, but to me it was both penetrating and symbolic. The image captured on film was that of a small Iraqi boy, about four or five years old, reaching high to shake hands with an American soldier who was guarding a barrier in a road somewhere in Iraq.

135

The small boy wore a baseball cap, slightly misaligned. His head was tilted to the side as he reached across the wrought iron barrier. The soldier, with his weapon shouldered, leaned forward slightly as he looked straight into the boy's eyes. The expression on the soldier's face was one of obvious appreciation and delight at the little boy's gesture of thanks and good will.

I was struck immediately by two different but related thoughts. The first was about the importance of having someone to look up to and follow, regardless of the circumstances. That thought, no doubt, emerged from the warmth of the scene created by the little boy's gesture. Even in the midst of the chaos of war, he gratefully looked up to his newly found hero.

My second thought was related to the importance of being modest and humble in the role of leader (and sometimes liberator). The soldier showed that sort of modesty and humility—it was written all over his face as he offered his hand to his new young friend.

As followers, we have an obligation to encourage our leaders and let them know how much we appreciate who they are and what they do. As followers, we have an obligation to provide meaningful feedback to our leaders. As followers, we have an obligation to catch our leaders doing things well and let them know we know, rather than focusing just on their shortcomings. I am always concerned about those in the highest levels of leadership in our country who are sitting ducks for nearly nonstop criticism of virtually everything they do, yet are seldom praised for what they do well. Meaningful feedback requires balance. When is the last time you let a leader know how much you appreciate his or her efforts? When is the last time you pointed out the useful and meaningful actions of a leader, as opposed to criticizing each stumble he or she may have made?

As leaders, we have an obligation to live up to the responsibilities of leadership. As leaders, we must be both humble and modest whenever we receive expressions of appreciation from followers. As leaders, we must be empathetic, patient, and thankful when followers are courageous enough to point out growth opportunities to us, keeping in mind that the things we least want to hear are those that we most need to hear.

Leadership and followership are an interesting and complex symbiosis. At the most elementary level, leaders cannot lead without followers and followers are always looking for their leader. But being the leader or the follower may vary from day to day or from situation to situation. Because the best leaders are also the best followers, we must be good at both, know when to do each, and have a genuine appreciation for the other at all times. Regardless of how effective we might think we are as leaders, we will surely find ourselves occasionally being in the situation depicted by the small Iraqi boy, needing someone to look up to, someone to follow, someone to emulate.

On those occasions, will we have the courage to follow? When we find ourselves in the role of leader, will we be worthy of being called a leader? Will we have earned the name by having served and sacrificed on behalf of others? Will we be guilty of doing the right things right? Hopefully, the answer to each of these questions is a thoughtful and genuine "yes."

Observation

43

Daily Reminders

Here are some daily reminders to help us monitor our leadership effectiveness:

*L*oyalty to vision and loyalty to people are hallmarks of real leaders.
- *Am I loyal to my family, organization, vision, philosophy, and the people around me?*
- *Am I loyal to myself and what I stand for?*
- *Am I loyal to my value system?*

*E*mpathy is about listening with the ears in my head and the ears in my heart with the intent to truly understand what people are saying to me.
- *Am I honoring the person speaking to me by listening and truly hearing what they have to say?*
- *Am I listening to hear the words and sensing the feelings being conveyed to me?*

*A*gape' is the form of love that requires that I respect others simply because they are fellow human beings and therefore deserve to be treated with dignity.
- *Do my thoughts and actions toward others, including those people I find troublesome, reflect my dedication to agape'?*
- *Is my love sufficient to serve and sacrifice for them?*

Dedication to principles, dedication to others, dedication to duty and honor at all times and in all circumstances is a direct reflection of the understanding I have of my personal leadership responsibilities.

- *When others observe my actions, could they rightfully accuse me of being a dedicated, principle-centered role model?*
- *Am I dedicated to committing "unexpected acts of kindness?"*

Energy applied to my daily life and my desire to learn is a direct indication that I understand that my effectiveness as a leader depends on action and that lifelong learning is the only path to personal mastery.

- *Am I doing everything possible physically, mentally, socially, emotionally, and spiritually to generate the strength needed to be an energetic leader?*
- *Do I energetically serve the legitimate needs of others?*

Respect for the thoughts and ideas of others can set me apart from others who may not be open-minded.

- *Am I respectful of the thoughts, ideas, and feelings of others—and, therefore, respectful of them?*
- *Do I respectfully seek out the thoughts and ideas of others, learning in the process of honoring them?*

Strength and sensitivity may seem to be opposites, but in fact they are mutually supportive.

- *Am I strong in the face of difficult challenges while remaining sensitive to the feelings of others?*
- *Am I sufficiently courageous to show and express my feelings?*

*H*umility is the soul of greatness.
- *Do I humble myself before others, thereby granting them greatness?*
- *Am I elevating the wants, needs, desires, and aspirations of others to a level at least as high as my own?*

*I*ntegrity is doing what I say I will do and is also about being well balanced and whole as a person.
- *Do my actions reflect my words?*
- *Am I aligned inside and out?*
- *Do I act with a singularity of purpose?*
- *Am I true to myself?*
- *Do I consciously work at balancing the multiple roles I have?*

*P*assion is about the fire in my gut that makes me who I am.
- *Could others who believe they live in a cold, hard world see me as someone who builds fires?*
- *Could others rightfully see the fire in my gut as a bonfire?*

Observation

44

Lead from the Inside Out

No matter how much we study and research a topic, we can always learn from the next book we pick up, the next life experience we have, the next new person we meet. New revelations of all sorts are out there just waiting to be discovered or developed. How wonderful and fascinating that we have so many chances to keep learning and continuing to enrich our understanding of who we are, what we feel, and what we know.

For a number of years, I have firmly believed that leadership is about action, not position, and about results, not popularity (after all, leaders must often make tough decisions that are not always well received). In my own simplistic view, effective leaders are those who both serve others and exercise their personal will to influence others in a positive way, guided by a principle-centered value system. Each of these views of leadership makes sense, each gives us significant challenges to live by, and in composite each helps us to understand the importance of being a good example to those around us.

Recently, however, I have had the opportunity to discover a new (at least to me), yet very rich, definition of leadership that touches my heart in ways different than any of the others that I have felt so strongly about for years. After his twenty years of wrestling with the concept of leadership,

Kevin Cashman, author of *Leadership from the Inside Out*, admits that he has come to realize, "Leadership is genuine self-expression that creates value."

I must admit that his insight had a profound impact on me from the moment I read the words. But it has had an even greater impact on me as I have thought about how his understanding interrelates with so many other pieces of the effective leadership puzzle with which I have struggled.

The elegant simplicity of Cashman's definition is also complex. Genuine self-expression requires that we have more than just a casual knowledge of who we are and what we think, believe, and feel. While the "leadership is action, not position" view truly calls us to action, unless we have a growing and reasonably accurate understanding of our own personal internal compass, our actions may not measure up to the challenge to "create value." By simple deductive reasoning, if our actions are not creating or adding value, they must be taking away value.

Subtracting value can take on many forms. For example, let's assume a leader makes an unpopular decision. Is the decision unpopular because it might simply cause us to work a little harder, or is it unpopular because it fundamentally harms people or relationships? Does the decision attack the humanity of others or enhance it? Clearly, if the decision is unpopular because it harms people or relationships, value is subtracted. Similarly, if a decision truly harms anyone's humanity, value is diminished. But if a leader makes a tough call that causes folks to work a little harder, that outcome does not, in itself, either add or subtract value. If in making that decision, people in some way are lifted up, value could very well be added, even though they might have to exert a little extra effort.

Few actions, if any, are completely neutral for a leader, so either adding or subtracting value are essentially the only two outcomes. And let's not forget—decisions that are unpopular in the short term could become very popular in the long run.

Bolman and Deal (*Leading with Soul*) argue that leadership is rooted in community, and, therefore, is fundamentally rooted in relationships. If their proposition is true, and I believe it is, as leaders we cannot ignore the impact that our decisions have on the people involved. Look around at recent actions taken by just a few in the business world that have impacted countless millions. Look at the impact of policies and decisions made by some governments that devalue the humanity of their people. The genocide in Rwanda in 1991 is just one of many graphic examples.

To be truly effective leaders, our actions must be guided by a broad and growing understanding of who we are and what we stand for, and by a value system structured around profound truths such as honesty, integrity, justice, and the need to serve others. Even so guided, our decisions may still not be popular. But rather than results at all costs, we need to act with the firm intent of adding value to whatever the endeavor might be, and we are able to do so only when we act from the genuineness of our core.

Cashman concludes that no matter how difficult it might seem, we must "integrate character, values and results." Only when we do so will we actually begin the long journey to becoming the very best leader we are capable of being.

Observation

45

Don't Be Afraid to Ask for Help

In many ways, our lives as leaders are filled with a wide range of seeming contradictions and paradoxes that can make life quite confusing. Take, for example, the notion of leader as servant. Throughout much of history, we have considered a leader as the person at the top of a traditional organizational structure (pyramid) who makes and enforces the rules, and is served by everyone in the organization below him or her. However, such a mental model of leaders and organizations is not only outdated, it is also "wrong-headed."

The most effective leaders, we now know, are those who serve, not those who expect to be served, regardless of where they are in an organization. For a senior manager to truly be a leader, she/he must position herself/himself at the bottom of an inverted pyramid organizational structure, serving subordinates at all levels above. The true greatness of leaders lies in their willingness to humble themselves in front of those whom they serve (lead) [which is another example of the living paradox for leaders that I have written about elsewhere].

In the same paradoxical way, the strongest leaders of all are those who courageously and willingly admit their weaknesses. How often have we seen senior managers, who should be leaders in the truest sense, display an air of infallibility? If you think about it, such arrogant and often boastful behavior can be extremely dangerous. Putting ourselves into such a situation, I would suggest that not much imagination is required for us to see just how vulnerable we can be when we deceive ourselves about our strengths and weaknesses—and we all have many of both.

But if we are courageous enough to know and admit our weaknesses, we will wisely create ways to get input and feedback from others who are able to use their strengths to provide a safety net under our weakness. From personal experience, I know how often I have been guilty of deceiving myself about what I knew about a subject when in fact I knew little, and I made disastrous decisions as a result. Clearly, bad decisions can be made even with much accurate knowledge and information, but the likelihood of such outcomes is far greater when we choose to "shoot from the hip." I have also witnessed my share of others doing the same. And why would anyone do such a silly thing?

As I see it, we choose that dangerous path for at least two primary reasons. First, particularly when in a position of importance, we believe we must be the expert in our area of responsibility and be in control. This powerful drive can negatively impact our behavior by closing our minds and hearts to what others might know and contribute.

The second is that we lack the courage to admit to ourselves that we really do not know enough to make an informed decision—and (likely subconsciously) conclude that asking others for assistance must be a sign of weakness. Our pride gets in the way of doing the sensible thing, specifically, asking for help from others who may very well know more than we do about the issues at hand.

The very best leaders are the ones who know they do not know everything and have the courage to ask for advice. They willingly admit their deficiencies, look for input from those they trust, and weigh carefully the information they gather. Admitting our weaknesses does not reduce our effectiveness. Quite the contrary, admitting our weaknesses and asking for help from others is an outward expression of our authenticity, humility, and honesty. In short, admitting our weaknesses is likely to be the most genuine way of showing our true strength.

Pretending we are strong makes us weak but admitting we are weak makes us strong.

Observation

46

Get a Coach, Be a Coach

I was recently reminded of the importance of coaching and feedback while participating in what has become for me a minor passion. After a nearly thirty-five-year hiatus from golf, I started playing again and, with a great deal of surprise, found out that when I began anew, it did not take me long to get back to the level I played at when I gave up the game. (That statement alone should give you some indication of my golf game!) But soon I began to improve, recording scores much better than I did when playing as a high school and college student.

Needless to say, I was feeling pretty pleased with (and very smug about) my progress. But just as this new level of confidence started to feel good, the wheels fell off. For whatever reason, my swing and "ball striking" took a nosedive. As hard as I tried, little seemed to help. My shots were seldom going where I wanted them to or as far as I knew that I was capable of hitting them. I drifted back into all of the classic mistakes that plague most amateur golfers— lifting my head before hitting the ball, hitting the "big ball" (the Earth) before hitting the small (white) one, using only my upper instead of entire body to swing, slicing, hooking, etc, *ad nauseum*.

The point, as you may be wondering, is that in our enthusiasm and dedication to become or be good leaders (or improve our effectiveness), many of us struggle with

147

issues similar to the ones I described about my golf game. Sometimes we don't know that what we are doing is wrong, so we do it anyway because we think it is right.

There is a story about a young bride who was getting ready to cook her first Sunday roast beef dinner for her new husband. He watched with interest as she prepared the meat to be put in the oven—but was surprised when she took a knife, cut a small chunk off of each end, and threw them away. He asked why she did that and, without a moment's hesitation, she simply said that it is the way her mother taught her to do it. The new husband later asked his mother-in-law why she cut the ends of the beef roast before cooking it and, surprisingly, he got the same answer from her that he got from his wife. The practice still made no sense to him, so the next time he visited his wife's grandmother, he asked her the question, too. The grandmother looked quite surprised at the question. With a bit of a grin on her face, she shrugged her shoulders and blurted out, "Are they still doing that? I did it because my roaster was too small and the meat wouldn't fit, but it was the largest pan I had!"

Sometimes we know that what we are doing is not what we should be doing, but we do it anyway. Sometimes we know what we are supposed to do, but our execution is poor or clumsy. Sometimes we know what we are supposed to do, but choose something ineffective instead. And sometimes we stumble into getting all the pieces put together right, surprise ourselves at the outcome, and have no idea how or why we did it!

As long as we listen to no one but ourselves and choose not to ask questions or seek input, we are doomed when it comes to seeing our weaknesses and our mistakes. If we continue not to recognize that what we are doing is wrong or ineffective, we will continue to execute clumsily, we will continue to make wrong choices, and we will likely be unable to repeat successful ventures that we "lucked into." We may eventually figure out what it takes to be a genuine leader, but in the meantime we could be practicing bad habits that soon become deeply ingrained in our behavior.

Lots of sports and other types of coaches maintain that practicing bad habits makes you better at those bad habits — the result being that the bad habits are even more difficult to break. As an aside, my golf game did not improve even with many trips to the driving range because I was "grooving" bad habits, locking them into muscle memory. So what to do?

Coaching and feedback are two of the most valuable tools we can use to help us grow. Getting the perspective of someone we respect about our performance (whether it be our golf game or our leadership skills) helps us to more quickly identify what we need to work on to implement change. Being coached by someone who has worked tirelessly to get to the top of his or her game helps us to see how we might need to modify our behavior to be more effective. Actively listening to their advice and counsel can save us endless hours of anguish. Being able to take advantage of their insight could instantly accelerate our growth. Looking at ourselves through the eyes of others often provides us a view of ourselves to which we are blind.

Just as the very best golfers in the world, including Phil Mickelson, constantly get feedback and coaching to fine-tune their games, or to regain skills or the "touch" they may have lost over time, the very best leaders anxiously and energetically seek input from others about their personal effectiveness as well. More often than not, our effectiveness does not require a complete retooling; rather, it can be revitalized with just a few minor adjustments.

Maybe today is the day that each of us should make a commitment to find a mentor, peer mentor, or coach to provide us with objective feedback on our leadership. Maybe today is the day we should each delve deeply into our own hearts to do an objective assessment of the person we are at the core of our being. And while I am at it, maybe today is the day I need to find a teaching professional to help me raise my golf game to a higher level.

Observation

47

Learn from History, Don't Be Controlled by It

The way organizations and teams deal with their history is an interesting and complex phenomenon. Many choose to use their past, including their mistakes and failures, as roadmaps to guide their growth and development. Others, unfortunately, continue to live in the past, even at the expense of progress. The same is of true of individuals. The degree to which organizations and teams have successful leaders at all levels is one of the most important factors in determining whether history is used effectively or not.

We have often heard that learning from history is an important part of avoiding the mistakes made by those who came before us. Yet organizations, from academia and the not-for-profit sectors to government and private enterprise, find intriguing and creative ways to keep feuds alive, sometimes for decades. Some people have an amazing capacity to find ways to prevent themselves from working amicably with one another. And sad as it may be, some involved in long-term squabbles have forgotten how the relationship started its downward spiral.

Regardless of the cause, using events of the past as justification for not working effectively together today is a problem that keeps many organizations from operating at their peak. Even the "Hatfields and McCoys," the two families that feuded for more than a hundred years, recently concluded that they should bury the hatchet and learn to get along. Like it or not, productivity and the way people work together and treat each other are directly impacted (for better or worse) by past events and relationships. The quality of an organization's working environment is a direct indicator of cooperation, and cooperation is a key indicator of effective teamwork and productivity.

Can misunderstandings, mismatched expectations, broken promises, failing to do what we say we will do, selfishness, and a wide range of other disappointing and hurtful behaviors cause difficulty in the workplace (and elsewhere)? Absolutely! But choosing not to deal with such situations in a timely, appropriate, and sensitive manner is nearly always even more troublesome. Often, a simple, timely, and genuine apology is adequate to repair the damage. Sometimes, when a breach is substantive, more time and energy are required to mend fences. Regardless, when relationships are allowed to remain sour for long periods of time, seldom, if ever, do the problems or hurt feelings simply go away.

Leaders (at all levels) have a particularly important role to play in assuring quality relationships. They must be visible examples of forgiving spirits. They must be—and hold others— accountable, be courageous, and be action-oriented. If a leader is the cause of the problem, he/she must initiate the steps needed to make amends. In addition, leaders can and should be catalysts to help others work through difficulties. Leaders in managerial positions have a particularly important role to play in resolving issues that negatively impact their organization's performance.

Armbruster's Axiom #5 states: The longer we hold on to history, the longer history will hold us back. Hopefully, my point is clear. Instead of dwelling on the negatives or failures of the past, learn from them and move on, all the wiser. Organizations that choose to do so are the ones that excel; those that do not are the ones that spin their wheels or, worse, slip backwards.

The good news is that when we opt to learn from the problems of the past, rather than using them as an excuse (by dwelling on them and keeping them alive), we give our organizations and ourselves the impetus to grow and prosper, using history to help build a better present and create hope for an even better future.

Observation

48

Relax, Keep It Simple, Don't Force It

Arnold Palmer, one of the finest golfers to ever play the game, once commented, "Golf is deceptively simple and endlessly complicated. It satisfies the soul and frustrates the intellect. It is at the same time rewarding and maddening—it is without a doubt the greatest game mankind has ever invented." In so many ways, golf is like leadership. Simply substitute the word "golf" with "leadership" in Arnie's message, and the statement is still true.

Leadership is deceptively simple but endlessly complex. Leadership satisfies (and challenges) the soul but frustrates the intellect. Leadership is at the same time both rewarding and frustrating. But without question, leadership is one of the most demanding yet satisfying endeavors facing mankind.

Arnie tells us that the best way to hit a great shot (whether a drive off the tee, a fairway iron, a blast out of a sand trap, or a birdie putt) is to relax and swing smoothly and with ease, concentrating on a few basic tenets. Yet many golfers do just the opposite. They approach the ball with a great deal of tension in their legs, arms, and hands. They grip the club with white knuckles, as though they were hanging on to a rope for dear life. Then with a rapid take away, and even more rapid down swing, they try to hit the ball as hard as they can. All the tension, grip tightness, and knee-jerk type swinging of the club are fundamental violations of the basics. The normal result of doing one or more of the wrong

154

things is that we mis-hit a shot and land in a spot from which it will be hard to recover. Are there leadership lessons here? You bet.

Regardless of where we are called upon to lead, most of the time we are usually able to perform at our peak when we don't *force* it. We are usually at our best when we work hard but stay relaxed, and concentrate on the basics. For leaders, the basics include being highly focused and acting from a genuine sense of service, honesty, integrity, and courage. When leaders are guided by a clear vision and have dedicated followers who share that vision, they are able to accomplish much, often beyond anything that seems possible, and do so with ease. When guided by their hearts, leaders often find that leading is a simple pleasure, one that allows them to transcend difficulties and obstacles that others might find onerous. Leaders also find that some of their most noteworthy efforts come when they simply relax and are themselves

Let me be clear, however: There is nothing easy about golf and there is nothing easy about leadership, either. And in a sense of full disclosure, golfers have different levels of what some call "natural" talent, just as leaders do. That being said, the best golfers in the world work very hard at their trade, practicing many hours per day. They are ever vigilant about the impact of small changes in their swing, stance, follow-through, and concentration. The best golfers are always consciously looking for ways to fine-tune their game, as well.

As leaders, we, too, must understand that hard work is required to be effective. We, too, must be vigilant about the impact that even small changes in our behavior, attitude, motivations, and other aspects of our interactions with others can have on our effectiveness. We, too, should always be looking for ways to improve. We must never shy away from the hard work of leading. Unfortunately, far too many people who should be really fine leaders do little to learn or practice so they fall short of what followers should expect of them.

I ran across an old leadership proverb in John Maxwell's *The 21 Most Powerful Minutes in a Leader's Day* that is well worth reconsidering periodically. The proverb states: "He who thinketh he leadeth but hath no one following only taketh a walk."

Are we really leading—or are we simply taking a walk? The answer to this question might have a lot to do with how relaxed we are and how much we are dedicated to the basics.

Observation

49

Leaders Do Not Act Alone

Reasonably early in my experience as a manager (and aspiring leader) in the U.S. Geological Survey, I was taught a lesson that served me well for the remainder of my career in government and beyond. The lesson came during the performance review at the end of my first year as Georgia district chief (manager in charge of USGS's Water Resources Division's state office). My supervisor, a man who became a mentor, advisor, coach, colleague, and dear friend, handed me his written evaluation of my first-year performance in the job. As I quickly dropped my eyes to the summary rating box to see how I had done, I saw his mark and was immediately overjoyed. Bottom line: He rated my performance as "outstanding," the highest rating on the scale.

I was smugly thinking, *This is truly amazing! First year on the job and the boss rates my performance as highly as possible.* I sat there with my hat size increasing by the moment, only to realize that Jim was not saying a word about the rating. The longer I sat there, the more deafening the silence became. *Why isn't he saying something? Why no verbal follow-up to the written record?* Although, in reality, it is likely that no more than thirty seconds passed, to me the stillness seemed to last a very, very long time.

Finally, with merciful compassion, my wise teacher and friend broke the silence with the question, "How long do you think you can keep this up?"

As though the silence had not been uncomfortable enough, his question sent a chill through me. "I don't understand your question," was the best I could muster after thinking a while.

"Your performance has really been terrific this year, but how long do you think you can continue doing everything yourself?" was his follow-up.

Fortunately, I had the uncharacteristic (for me) good sense to say nothing for a while. Then he shared some sage advice: "It's not your job to do everything. It's your job to ensure everything gets done."

More silence. My brain and heart were racing, trying to digest his advice.

Although I had been a manager for several years prior to accepting the job in Georgia, I had not grasped until that moment that, as a manager and a leader, I was not supposed to do so much by myself. What I was being taught, compassionately, in that moment was that I was being challenged to give others the opportunity to take responsibility and shine. I was being asked to let go and trust others to do assignments that in my conceit I thought only I could do well and to give power away in order to increase the power vested in me. What a sobering and educational experience! (This entire incident was for me what noted psychologist Morris Massey calls "a significant emotional event.")

With all the energy I had, I finally mustered enough courage to look at Jim and say, most likely with a quiver in my voice, "I think I understand."

Although I have tried hard to observe his advice and make it a part of me, whether or not I have actually been successful in practicing Jim's advice over the long term is for others to judge. But, recently, I was thinking about that cathartic event for the hundredth time, and wondered how all of what happened that day relates to Kevin Cashman's observation (in *Leading from the Inside Out*) that "leadership is genuine self-expression to create (or add) value."

Cashman came to his conclusion several years after the event I have just described, so Jim could not have read the book. Just the same, he consciously or unconsciously taught me (thereby creating value in our relationship) the essence of Cashman's message — specifically, that I would be adding or creating value whenever I helped others to grow, whenever I trusted them, and when they felt genuinely empowered by my actions toward them. He taught me that I could only be a real leader when I gave away power rather than hoarding it, and that I would only be an effective leader when I added or created value for others. He did not use Cashman's words, but he did convey every ounce of Cashman's message.

We cannot be the judges of our own success. Only others can do that for us. But we can (and should) evaluate how others have added or created value to our lives, like Jim and so many others have enriched mine. Maybe now is a good time to reflect back and acknowledge how others have helped us to be more effective leaders.

- Who has added value by listening empathetically?
- Who had the courage to tell me when I was off track?
- Who provided me encouragement when I was struggling?
- Who helped me move forward when I was stuck?
- Who loved me when I was not particularly lovable?
- Who was loyal when times were tough and others were critical?
- Who accepted me for whom and what I am even when that was difficult?
- Who gave me opportunities to shine when the challenge seemed beyond my reach?
- Who provided advice, then let me choose how I would use it?

Even the very best leaders are not effective when acting solely on their own. Their effectiveness is heavily dependent on those with whom they choose to surround themselves. For those who have taken you under their wing, are you adding value to them by what you say and do? And who have you chosen to be your closest associates and thus help you grow as a leader, even as you help them?

Observation

50

Resilience Is Required to Overcome Adversity

No doubt you may have noticed that not everything we attempt in life turns out as we would have hoped. If you are anything at all like me, you have experienced significant disappointments in both your personal and professional life, even when doing your dead-level best, because of circumstances beyond your control.

You may also have experienced disappointment with yourself because of choices you made that, if given the opportunity to do over, you would choose differently. An important lesson we would all do well to learn and practice is to rebound with new levels of energy no matter how often we slip, stumble, fall, embarrass, or disappoint ourselves and those who count on us.

Resilience is a major factor in determining just how successful we are at doing whatever we attempt. Resilience has served individuals, leaders, organizations, countries, and civilizations well throughout history and will quite definitely serve us well today as we are jostled about by the circumstances of the chaotic world in which we live.

Winston Churchill clearly knew the importance of resilience. Now considered by many historians as one of the finest, most influential leaders in modern history, Churchill appropriately gained that reputation, in part, because of his dogged determination and unwillingness to allow setbacks to defeat him. Never before had England been under such a massive attack as the one unleashed upon her by Germany during World War II. As he stepped forward to guide England through one of the most devastating periods of her existence, Churchill graphically showed his countrymen, friends, the enemy, and the world that he was an amazing and resilient leader.

While involved in public service for much of his life through the military and later through politics, Churchill was not always considered the powerful and important leader he ultimately grew to be. Rather, he was more like a "leader-in-the-making" who matured just in time to become the kind of prime minister England would need in her darkest hours. With his country under direct attack, Churchill often spoke directly to his countrymen over the radio. He courageously preached a message of encouragement and determination. But on one occasion, in spite of an extremely demanding schedule, Churchill chose to accept an invitation to speak in person—he agreed to make the commencement address to the Oxford University class of 1944. The assembled students were likely the very brightest young minds in all of Great Britain, so he surely considered carefully the words of his message.

After a proper introduction, Churchill stood, walked to the podium, surveyed the bright and anxious young people seated before him, and delivered what some consider one of his finest speeches.

"Never give up!" he began. He paused for quite some time then continued, "Never give up!" After a much longer pause, he looked into their eyes again and concluded his message to them, "Never give up!" Having passionately and forcefully delivered what he considered to be the most important advice he could give the graduates, he returned to his chair and sat down.

My guess is that there were some who felt cheated by the brevity and repetition of the three-word message.

But surely there were many who realized that Churchill's admonition was not only vital for them and their homeland at that moment, but that it would serve them equally well in the future, regardless of what they opted to do with their lives.

In our growth and development as leaders, we would do well to adopt Churchill's message as a mantra. There is a bad news-good news story here, though. The bad news is that no matter how hard we work, no matter how hard we try to be effective leaders, we will occasionally come up short, and occasionally fail—miserably. The good news, however, is we get to choose how we respond. Will we allow disappointment, mistakes, and failures to tarnish our enthusiasm (all of which diminish our ability to lead), or will we choose to follow Churchill's advice, "Never give up," and try again and again?

Making mistakes as leaders is a vital part of our growth process because if we are not making some, we are likely spending entirely too much time in our comfort zone. So if we are really serious about growing as leaders, and surely making our share of mistakes along the way, we will have numerous opportunities to regroup and start over. Our steadfastness to overcome adversity and move forward measures our resilience and is a very useful metric to assess our development. Are you ready to adopt a "never give up," resilient leadership attitude?

Observation

51

Who Are You? Where Are You Going? Why Are You Going There?

In his book *Leadership from the Inside Out*, Kevin Cashman relates the story of a priest who was confronted by a soldier while walking down a road in pre-revolutionary Russia. The soldier, aiming his rifle at the priest, commanded, "Who are you? Where are you going? Why are you going there?" Unfazed, the priest calmly replied, "How much do they pay you?"

Somewhat surprised, the soldier responded, "Twenty-five kopecks a month."

The priest paused then in a deeply thoughtful manner said, "I have a proposal for you. I'll pay you fifty kopecks each month if you will stop me here every day and challenge me to respond to *those same three questions*."

As I got to the end of this story, I was smiling externally at the simplicity of the message, yet was internally perplexed at the significant complexity of these three questions. In composite, *Who are you? Where are you going?* and *Why are you going there?* should force us to focus on some of the most fundamental issues that we deal with as leaders—or, for that matter, as human beings! Together these three simple questions, if taken seriously, should challenge us to question the purpose of our lives.

Oftentimes when asked who we are, we tend to focus on the job we do, the title on our business card, or the honor we may have just received. But is that *really* who we are? I think not. When thinking about who we are, we would be far better served by thinking about the core of our being, the essence of our character, the motivations that drive our actions, and the roots of our feelings. Granted, the job we do is important, but it is only a job and they come and go. New business cards are regularly printed to reflect job changes. And the honor that was just conferred, while clearly something to celebrate, fades with time.

By contrast, our core or essence, our character and our motivations are always with us and are always being challenged by the circumstances of the world around us. By regularly spending time in careful, thoughtful self-examination, we can get and stay more fully in touch with who we are inside.

Please understand that self-reflection is not a static, one-time affair—we must repeat the process over and over as we learn and grow. Really getting to know ourselves may well be one of the most difficult challenges we face in life because doing so requires honesty, courage, and humility. Doing so, however, is powerful medicine.

A friend recently told me of his admiration for George Washington Carver, the amazing black scientist who worked tirelessly to understand the nutritional, commercial, and medical uses of the peanut. In January 1921, Carver and a number of other scientists from around the country were called to Washington, D.C., to testify before Congress about their work. Because he was black, they called Carver last, letting him sit and wait in the hallway—for three days.

As he was finally entering into the hearing room, one committee member, in a cowardly attempt to belittle Carver, said in a sufficiently loud voice that all could hear, "I suppose you have plenty of peanuts and watermelon to make you happy."

Carver was tempted to turn around, walk out, and go home without testifying. But in his biography, he said,

"Whatever they said of me, I knew that I was a child of God and so I said to myself inwardly, 'Almighty God, let me carry out your will.'"

To make matters worse, after Carver had made the long trip from Alabama and after he waited for three days, the committee announced that he had twenty minutes to report on his research. Twenty minutes! But when his twenty minutes went by so quickly, they allotted him another twenty minutes, then another, and so on. Eventually his testimony lasted several hours and at the end, everyone in the room, including the entire committee, stood and gave him a raucous round of applause.

Knowing who you are gives you the strength to endure almost anything. George Washington Carver truly knew who he was, was comfortable with himself, and drew significant courage and strength from that knowledge — as all leaders can if they try.

When asked where we are going, we often respond with an answer that focuses on our current destination or short-term goals, rather than addressing the more fundamental question about where our life is headed. That is not surprising, though, since the first question is clearly much easier to answer than the second. Answering the more difficult question requires us to describe a vision for our life, a focus that is so profound that it shapes our thoughts, feelings, motivations, and behavior. Many of us struggle to set such a course even when we know at a visceral level that vision helps us to make tough choices in the midst of turmoil. So many of us actually spend more time deciding where to go on vacation than we spend on the far more important decision about where we should go in life.

The third and final question that the priest offered to pay the soldier to ask him each day ("Why are you going there?") is about our motivations and meaning — logical perspectives beyond the fundamentals of who we are and

166

what contributions we want to make in life. Is our motivation about self-gratification? Is about lifting ourselves up at the expense of others? Is it about trying to make ourselves look good in the eyes of others? Is it about getting our needs met? Or is it about our genuine desire to love (*agape'*) and to serve the legitimate needs of others and to make selfless contributions to our families, organizations, communities, and humankind in general? This question is quite complicated and requires that our intentions be coupled with our choice to act. Mahatma Gandhi commented, "The difference between what we do and what we are capable of doing would suffice to solve most of the world's problems."

I would simply add that in taking the actions we are capable of taking, we should concentrate our energy first on being significant on the one-on-one scale. When we concentrate our energies there, we will soon begin to see we are making a difference in the lives of others on a much larger scale. So the final challenge of living out our responses to the three simple questions originally posed by the soldier comes down to our willingness to act on our intentions, to live our vision.

So...*Who are you? Where are you going? Why are you going there?*

Observation

52

Be a Servant

⎯⎯⎯⎯⎯⎯⎯⎯⎯⎯⎯⎯⎯⎯⎯⎯

Leadership is steeped in service. And at the very core of our leadership responsibility is the challenge to identify the legitimate needs of others. But simply identifying those needs is not sufficient. As leaders, we must act on what we know and, possibly more importantly, we must act on what we feel.

In short, real leaders are the ones who serve and sacrifice on behalf of others. They are the ones who understand that in sacrificing for someone by reaching beyond themselves, they must often give up something; they must pay some price. Sacrifice is not a sacrifice unless it costs you something — time, energy, influence, resources, etc. *Sacrifice* is about reaching outside of ourselves for the purpose of easing someone else's burden.

In his *The 21 Irrefutable Laws of Leadership*, John Maxwell says, "Sacrifice is a constant in leadership. It is an ongoing process, not a one-time payment... The circumstances may change from person to person, but the principle doesn't. Leadership means sacrifice." At the risk of losing sight of another related issue, effective leaders also graciously allow others to serve and sacrifice for them, but neither demand nor expect to be served.

Intellectually, these ideas are relatively simple to conceptualize and, emotionally, these feelings are simple to internalize, but both are far more difficult to act upon. Borrowing from a popular metaphor, many are the slips between the knowing and the doing. Many are the opportunities that we fail to recognize the needs of others and thus fail to act. Many are the occasions when we simply do not muster what it takes to do what is right. Many are the times we give in to the temptation to do what is easy rather than stepping up to the plate by accepting significant challenges.

Former Senator Paul Simon wrote an article published in the October 31, 2003, issue of the *Chronicle of Higher Education*—the opening paragraph of which gets to the heart of the matter:

> Today leaders in all areas—politics, media, religion, and education—are guilty of giving in to what is easy instead of fighting for what is right. We have "leadership" that does not lead, that panders to our whims rather than tells us the truth, that follows the crowd rather than challenges us, that weakens us rather than challenges us. It is easy to go downhill, and we are now following that easy path. Pandering is not illegal, but it is immoral. It is doing the convenient when the right course demands inconvenience and courage.

Serving and sacrificing for others requires that we act positively and decisively even when doing so is not convenient. We must be willing to do the moral thing even when doing so requires every ounce of courage that we might have in our being—and then a little more. But we each have the ability, power, and wherewithal do the right thing regardless of the circumstances. We each have the capability of rising above what Senator Simon refers to as the easier path of pandering. We each have the ability to tell the truth, even though doing so is difficult. A very young but very wise Anne Frank said, "How wonderful it is that nobody need wait a single moment before starting to improve the world."

The idea of improving the world might seem a bit overwhelming, even for an experienced leader. It clearly is an awesome task. Yet our service to and sacrifice for others are at the heart of our challenge to lead. Serving just one person, in some small way, is a very real and tangible way for us to improve the world around us. Each of us can do that, and we have many opportunities each day.

For example, we serve another when we are fully present to them, giving of our time and attention. We are another's servant when we choose to devote our personal energy to help someone in need. We serve when we use our influence to help another without regard for being recognized for our efforts. We serve and sacrifice when we help others to grow to reach their potential. And we also serve when we sacrificially give of our resources to help those less fortunate than ourselves, especially when we do so anonymously. John Maxwell suggests in his *The 21 Most Powerful Minutes in a Leader's Life* that for us to really achieve our full leadership potential, we must not only "give up to go up" and "give up to grow up," we must also "give up to stay up."

With that in mind, I pose this rather simple yet complex question: How much are you willing to give up to increase your leadership effectiveness?

Epilogue

The Power of Leading with Aggressive Humility

When I began writing this series of observations on leadership more than five years ago, I had no plan to publish it so I gave no thought to how the collection would end. The last entry would be the end. But colleagues, family, and friends began to encourage me to compile and share these thoughts, so I had to face the music—what you start, you have to finish.

Most of the observations contained in this collection were finished more than three years ago, but I did nothing to complete the work because, frankly, I did not know how to finish. Finally, having to make a decision about closure, I felt in my heart that the final pages either needed to provide a summary of the major thoughts conveyed by the chapters or at least leave the reader with a take-away message that would be a real *brain worm*—one of those ideas that hangs around in the thought process and maybe even nags you in some useful way. But the last entry kept evading me. Then, I heard a sermon topic and knew instantly how to end this volume. Here is the foundation for my thinking about what guides true leadership. I hope it will nag you, too.

All truly meaningful leadership—whether in the workplace, the home, the community, or church—is founded on fundamental, universal principles. These principles, I believe, are scriptural and were taught by Christ himself. True leadership is about serving others, not being served. I don't know if my evolving concepts of leadership were shaped by my spiritual, moral beliefs, or whether I discovered how they aligned with my spiritual beliefs after I began putting them on paper, but for me they are intimately woven together.

I meet with a group of men at my church (I am Roman

171

Catholic) most Friday mornings when I am in town. We rotate the responsibility for giving a twenty-five-minute or so reflection on a topic of our choice. About half a dozen times a year, the presentation falls to me. Being the lazy person I am, I frequently use one of the observations presented here and shamelessly reuse ideas for those talks. Almost without exception, if I substitute the word "Christian" for each time "leadership" appears in one of the lessons I had written earlier, I have the basis for my talk.

I share these thoughts with you because I feel it important that you, the reader, understand that I am heavily influenced by my faith, that I do my best to live by Christ's teachings, and that I can only lead based on who and what I am. As someone striving to do the right thing in all situations, but who often stumbles and makes mistakes, I am a work in progress. But no matter what religious persuasion you might be, these leadership principles can be applied anywhere, anytime.

In June 2007, I participated in a mission trip to Honduras, along with about two dozen others from my church. We worked with the Franciscan Friars of the Renewal in Comayagua, and had the honor of working with many wonderful people from the local area, particularly those at an orphanage the friars serve. As missionaries, we began each day with mass. One morning, Father John Anthony, chief servant (local head of the friars), preached a sermon that he entitled "Aggressive Humility." He had hardly begun his homily when I realized just how this book must end.

My understanding of the importance of humility continues to evolve, so none of my earlier writings on the topic catch the deeper meaning of the word. I have believed for some time that humility may very well be the most important virtue of all for effective leadership. This opinion galvanized for me when I heard Father John Anthony speak, though I did not fully understand it at that moment. I was startled to have the meaning of the word humility suddenly take on new dimensions when combined with the concept of being "aggressive." And what a revelation to understand that true leadership is founded on aggressive humility!

You might be thinking that *aggressive* and *humility* are contrary terms, but, in fact, they are not. One of Webster's definitions of *aggressive* is to be "assertive or militant." *Militant* certainly does not seem to fit in this notion of aggressive humility; rather, it seems to creates even more of a dichotomy. But Webster clarifies that *militant*, while implying a fighting disposition, really suggests an attitude that is not self-seeking but rather extremely devoted to a cause. The term *aggressive*, then, can very realistically apply to passionate dedication to a cause, even a noble cause.

The virtue of humility is defined in the *Catholic Encyclopedia* as, "A quality by which a person, considering his own defects, has a lowly opinion of himself and willingly submits himself to God and to others for God's sake." St. Bernard of Clairveaux, a twelfth-century intellectual giant, defined humility as, "A virtue by which a man knowing himself as he truly is, abases himself." Both of these definitions coincide with that given by St. Thomas Aquinas: "The virtue of humility consists in keeping oneself within one's own bounds, not reaching out to things above one, but submitting to one's superior."

Father Thomas Williams, dean of theology at the Regina Apostolorum Pontifical University in Rome, and Vatican correspondent for NBC and MSNBC, says in his book, *Spiritual Progress*:

> Humility is the virtue that sifts through the many paradoxes of human existence in search of the truth. It peels off the layers of vanity and self-deception to reveal us to ourselves, as we really are. And it does so not by comparing us to other people to see

173

how we stack up in the rogue's gallery of humanity but by placing us before the throne of God.... The truly humble person sees himself as he really is, since he sees himself as God sees him.

With this explanation, Father Williams provides a similar description of the connection between humility and truth, as C. S. Lewis did in his heavily acclaimed *Screwtape Letters*.

The *Screwtape Letters* is a series of letters written by a journeyman devil named "Screwtape," which he sent to his nephew, a devil-in-training named "Wormwood." Screwtape passes along his devilish wisdom to Wormwood in his letters so that Wormwood can lead his patient or client down the path of moral destruction. In one of those letters, Screwtape says

I see only one thing to do at the moment. Your patient has become humble; have you drawn his attention to the fact? All virtues are less formidable to us once the man is aware that he has them, but this is especially true of humility. Catch him at the moment when he is really poor in spirit and smuggle into his mind the gratifying reflection, "By Jove! I'm being humble," and almost immediately pride—pride at his own humility—will appear. If he awakes to the danger and tries to smother this new form of pride, make him proud of his attempt.

Screwtape further advises Wormwood:

The great thing is to make him (the patient) value an opinion for some quality other than truth, thus introducing an element of dishonesty and make-believe into the heart of what otherwise threatens to become a virtue. By this method thousands of humans have been brought to think that humility means pretty women trying to believe they are ugly and clever men trying to believe they are fools. The Enemy (God) wants to bring the man to a state of mind (in) which he could design the best cathedral in the world, and know it to be the best, and rejoice in the fact, without being any more (or less) or otherwise glad at having done it than he would be if it had been done by another.

So, humility, particularly the humility exercised by leaders, is based on the truth—the truth about God, the truth about the talents that God has given us, the honest truth about our shortcomings. Seems simple enough, doesn't it? But there are significant barriers between us and the truth, including pride, vanity, arrogance, and self-righteousness. All of a sudden, the diversions that keep us from being humble are a formidable minefield. As we climb our ladders of success, we stray into this minefield with no idea we are there. When this happens, leadership effectiveness suffers in direct proportion to how deeply we are mired in the minefield.

All of us like to be recognized for what we do. But some of us want to be praised constantly. And a few of us are compelled to look for admiration from others to boost our sense of who we are. But if we hope to be humble, we must strip ourselves of such pride because pride is about looking inward, whereas humility is about looking outward. I heard a wonderful expression recently that reveals why so many of us have such a hard time being humble: "I might not be much, but I'm all I think about."

One of the most significant, lifelong personal struggles I have had is that of overcoming pride—the unhealthy kind of pride that leads one to believe that he is more important, that his ideas are better, that he deserves the promotion more, that his counsel is wiser, that his needs and aspirations are more important than those around him. Such pride leads us to treat others with disrespect, to climb over colleagues who get in our way, to be unwilling to share what we know with others, and to smother the imagination and enthusiasm of others so we can be the brightest star.

Prideful behavior blocks the path to humility that God asks us to trod and which is required of us to be servant-leaders. Such conduct as being unwilling to admit mistakes and the tendency to judge others keep us from becoming the leaders we aspire to be. We usually find it much easier to find faults in the words and actions of others than to make courageous admissions of our own shortcomings. Remember Jesus' admonition: Remove the log from your own eye before removing the speck from your brother's eye.

There are many useful ways of looking at humility, but at the core of each definition is the sense of reaching outside of ourselves for a greater purpose—to empty ourselves. Scott Hahn, a professor at Franciscan University, described humility in a recent television presentation as, "Loving service to others." Such a simple yet profound message. This description—like the definitions mentioned earlier—sounds like it should be reserved for use at home, with our family, in our church community, in theological dialogue. But, in fact, this definition (as well as the others) fits well in the workplace, in the boardroom, in leadership development programs, and in executive coaching sessions. Loving service to others is the same love that Jesus promulgated when He said to "love your enemies," that *agape'* form of love, the unconditional treating of another with dignity and respect regardless of what they say or do.

Loving service to others is simple when others are lovable. The challenge, of course, is when they are not. As leaders, we face difficult situations and even more difficult people, so our challenges are many. The underpinning for the way we choose to treat others is humility.

So far, I defined humility, talked some about the

concept of being aggressive, and described how humility can be compromised, but I have not talked about "aggressive humility." Let me attempt to connect the dots between these two words with several equations.

Humility = Loving service to others
True love = *Agape'* (or 'unconditional' love)
Aggressive = Militant
Militant = Passionate devotion to a cause

Therefore,

Aggressive humility = Passionate, unconditional devotion to the loving service of others

There are a number of examples of passionate devotion to the unconditional service of others. For Christians, the most obvious example is Jesus' death on the cross for our sins. Christians believe that He suffered and died for us. How coincidental that the word we use to describe the humiliation and suffering Jesus bore for us is "passion." He could have easily bypassed the passion, He could have bypassed the crucifixion and death, but instead He passionately gave Himself for us and for our eternal salvation.

More recently, there is Mother Teresa of Calcutta. She was passionate and she was devoted to caring for the poorest of the poor. Even the most hardened cynic would have to admit that Mother Teresa was aggressively humble in her passionate devotion to caring for the needs of those forgotten in the gutters of Calcutta and other parts of the world.

These two examples are the tip of the iceberg. We have a rich history of many selfless people who have gone before us or who may still be living with us today. But the real challenge for us as leaders is this: What can we personally do to be aggressively humble?

To jump-start our understanding of what it means to be humble, imagine what it might be like to have lost all pride in everything. In Atlanta, Georgia, where I live, there are tens of thousands of people who have lost everything, or never had anything, who live on the streets, in stairways, under bridges, etc. As an eye-opener, imagine what it would be like to have so little that the only warm place you could find to sleep is in the corner of a public rest room. What would it be like to offer your morning or evening prayers with little to no hope in sight?

With all semblances of pride wiped away, humility is what is left. You may know that the word *humility* is from the Latin root word *humus*, meaning "ground" or "soil." We humans are from the earth. The closer we are to the ground metaphorically, the closer we come to being humble. This is particularly true of leaders because leaders must be role models in all they do.

So, here are a few suggestions for enhancing our leadership potential by pursing humility aggressively:

- Make it a practice to know those who empty your office trash can, sweep the floor, and clean the restrooms. Treat them with the same dignity and respect you would a dear friend.

- When you have a disagreement with someone, even if you are only one-tenth of one percent at fault, be the first to offer an apology. Doing so accelerates reconciliation and provides an example to others.

- Be as kind and friendly with the lowest-level person in your organization as you would with your boss' boss. I am always chagrined to see folks forget their friends as they climb the corporate ladder. (As an aside, some would say the quality of any organization can be judged by how the lowest person on the totem pole is treated.)

- Be quick to recognize and give credit to God for your talents, successes, and gifts. Without those gifts, anything we do would not be possible anyway, so be truthful.

- Avoid being kind and generous just so that others might have a higher opinion of us—doing so saps value of our good deeds before God. Jesus admonished us that the right hand should not be aware of what the left hand is doing. Treat everyone with dignity and respect without looking for something in return.
- Pray the Litany of Humility regularly (even if you are not a religious person) because it will remind you of the many blind spots that lead to pride. Also, remember that each incantation in the litany represents a form of humiliation that was inflicted upon Jesus himself while He was on Earth, which we are subject to as well. (If you are unfamiliar with it, simply Google "Litany of Humility.")
- Dedicate time, energy, and prayer to thinking more about the needs of others and far less about your personal needs. Psychologists have long known that one of the best treatments for depression is to think and act outside of ourselves.
- Think about yourself less rather than thinking less of yourself. Doing so will allow you to concentrate more energy on recognizing and taking action on behalf of those that need your help because your ego will not get in the way.
- No matter who you are with, make it a point to be 100 percent present to them. When you do, you are choosing to think of them first, not yourself, and by so doing you lift them up. As simple as this might sound, being fully present to others is really quite difficult!
- If you must take disciplinary action as a manager or as a parent, be hard on the actions, soft on others' dignity.
- Praise others selflessly and accept feedback courageously and graciously. As managers and leaders, our success

is often a reflection of the hard work of those around us so always share the credit. When others provide us feedback, they provide us a way of viewing ourselves through their eyes. Thank them graciously for their courage and candor.

* Keep the needs of others in the forefront of your thinking. I recently told my son I would pray for him as he faced a difficult conversation with a colleague the next day. He thanked me and accepted the offer. Then he asked that I pray for his colleague, too — such a small request, but what a huge indicator of an aggressively humble spirit. He taught me much through his request.

My understanding and practice of aggressive humility is in its infancy. But I am fully convinced that aggressive humility is what God requires of me as a Christian. I am also convinced that all leaders must practice aggressive humility if they expect to be effective. Do you have the courage to look truthfully at yourself, your actions, your thoughts and feelings? Do you have the courage it takes to lead with aggressive humility? If so, you might very well be on the way to being a leader. But along your way, look around, watch, listen, observe — learn.

Enjoy the journey!

Work Cited

Autry, James A. *The Servant Leader*. Roseville, California: Prima Publishing, 2001.

Bennis, Warren. *Managing People Is Like Herding Cats*. Provo, Utah: Executive Excellence Publishing, 1997.

Blank, Warren. *The 9 Natural Laws of Leadership*. New York, New York: American Management Association: 1995.

Bolman, Lee G., and Deal, Terrence E. *Leading with Soul*. San Francisco, California: Josey-Bass, Inc., Publishers, 2002.

Cashman, Kevin. *Leadership from the Inside Out*. Provo, Utah: Executive Excellence Publishing, 1998.

Cashman, Kevin. *Awakening the Leader Within*. Hoboken, New Jersey: John Wiley & Sons, Inc., 2003.

Covey, Stephen R. *The 7 Habits of Highly Effective People*. New York, New York: Simon & Schuster, 1989

Crosby, Philip B. *Quality is Free*. New York, New York: McGraw-Hill, Inc., 1979.

De Pree, Max. *Leadership Is an Art*. New York, New York: Dell Publishing, a division of Bantam Doubleday Dell Publishing Group, Inc., 1989.

De Pree, Max. *Leadership Jazz*. New York, New York: Dell Publishing, a division of Bantam Doubleday Dell Publishing Group, Inc., 1992.

Drucker, Peter F., in Hasselbein, Frances; Goldsmith, Marshall; and Beckhard, Richard, editors. *The Leader of the Future*. San Francisco, California: Josey-Bass Publishers, 1996.

Fulghum, Robert L. *Everything I Ever Needed to Know in Life I Learned in Kindergarten*. New York, New York: The Random House Publishing Group, a division of Random House, Inc., 1986

Work Cited

Gardner, John W. *On Leadership*. New York, New York:
The Free Press, a Division of Simon & Schuster, 1990.

Goleman, Daniel. *Emotional Intelligence*. New York, New
York: A Bantam Book, a division of Bantam
Doubleday Dell Publishing Group, Inc., 1995.

Kouzes, James M. and Posner, Barry Z. *Credibility*. San
Francisco, California: Josey-Bass, Inc. Publishers,
1993.

Kouzes, James M., and Posner, Barry Z. *The Leadership
Challenge*. San Francisco, California: Josey-Bass, Inc.
Publishers, 2002.

Kun, Jeanne, editor. *Love Songs—Wisdom from Saint
Bernard of Clairvaux*. Ijamsville, New Jersey: The
Word Among Us Press, 2001.

Greenleaf, Robert K. *Servant Leadership*. Mahwah, New
Jersey: The Paulist Press, 1977.

Hunter, James C. *The Servant*. New York, New York:
Crown Business, Member of Crown Publishing
Group, a division of Random House Inc., 1998.

Land, George, and Jarman, Beth. *Breakpoint and
Beyond—Mastering the Future*. New York, New York:
HarperBusiness, a Division of HarperCollins
Publishers, 1992.

Lewis, C. S. *Screwtape Letters*. New York, New York:
HarperCollins Publishers, Inc., 1942.

Manz, Charles C. *The Leadership Wisdom of Jesus*. San
Francisco, California: Barrett-Koehler Publishers, Inc.,
1998.

Maxwell, John C. *The 21 Most Powerful Minutes in a
Leader's Day*. Nashville, Tennessee: Thomas Nelson
Publishers, Inc., 2000.

Maxwell, John C. *The 21 Irrefutable Laws of Leadership*.
Nashville, Tennessee: Thomas Nelson Publishers, Inc.,
2002.

Patterson, Kerry; Grenny, Joseph; McMillan, Ron; and Switzler, Al. *Crucial Conversations*. New York, New York: McGraw Hill, a division of The McGraw-Hill Company, 2002.

Peck, M. Scott, *The Road Less Traveled*. New York, New York: Simon & Schuster, 1978.

Senge, Peter M. *The Fifth Discipline*. New York, New York: Currency Doubleday, a division of Bantam Doubleday Dell Publishing Group, Inc., 1990.

Simon, Paul. *A GI Bill for Today*. Chronicle of Higher Education: October 31, 2003.

Snyder, C. R. *The Will and the Ways: Development and Validation of an Individual-Differences Measure of Hope*. Journal of Personality and Social Psychology, Volume 60, Issue 4, April 1991.

Staub, Robert E. II. *The Heart of Leadership*. Provo, Utah: Executive Excellence Publishing, 1996.

Staub, Robert E. *The Seven Acts of Courage*. Provo, Utah: Executive Excellence Publishing, 1999.

The Arbinger Institute. *Leadership and Self-Deception*. San Francisco, California: Barrett-Koehler Publishers, Inc., 2000.

Williams, Thomas D. *Spiritual Progress*. New York, New York: Hachette Book Group, U.S.A., 2007.

Yokoyama, John, and Michelli, Joseph. *When Fish Fly*. New York: Hyperion, 2004.

Zander, Rosamund Stone, and Zander, Benjamin. *The Art of Possibility*. Boston, Massachusetts: Harvard Business School Press, 2000.

About the Author

Jeff Armbruster is Senior Consultant, Armbruster & Associates, LLC. For the past 8 years, he has provided customized training, coaching, and consulting services to a wide range of clients in government, the private sector, research institutes, academia, and not-for-profit organizations. Jeff offers energetic guidance, support and encouragement to organizations interested in significantly higher levels of performance, particularly in the areas of principle-centered leadership, emotional intelligence, teamwork effectiveness, and one-on-one executive coaching.

Jeff retired from the U.S. Geological Survey in August 2001, with more than 37 years of service. During his career with USGS, he spent 15 years working in the field of hydrology (he has both a BS and MS in Civil Engineering) and 20 years managing scientific research programs. During his final 2 years, he served as a member of the USGS's Executive Leadership Team and served as one of the director's senior policy advisors.

Jeff lives in Norcross, Georgia, with his wife and best friend, Laurel. They have two children, both married, and 3 grandchildren, so far! In his leisure time, he enjoys traveling, woodworking, reading, and playing golf.